To Doreen

December 2010

Backyard Bird Sounds

FRED VAN GESSEL

First published in 2015 by Reed New Holland Publishers Pty Ltd
London • Sydney • Auckland

The Chandlery, Unit 704, 50 Westminster Bridge Road,
London SE1 7QY, United Kingdom
1/66 Gibbes Street, Chatswood, NSW 2067, Australia
5/39 Woodside Avenue, Northcote 0627, Auckland, New Zealand

www.newhollandpublishers.com

Copyright © 2015 Reed New Holland Publishers Pty Ltd
Copyright © 2015 in text: Fred van Gessel
Copyright © 2015 in sounds: Fred van Gessel
Copyright © 2015 in photographs: individual photographers as credited on page 58

All rights reserved. No part of this publication may be reproduced, stored in a retrieval system or transmitted, in any form or by any means, electronic, mechanical, photocopying, recording or otherwise, without the prior written permission of the publishers and copyright holders.

A record of this book is held at the British Library and the National Library of Australia.

ISBN 978 1 92151 745 7

Managing Director: Fiona Schultz
Publisher and Project Editor: Simon Papps
Designer: Thomas Casey
Production Director: Olga Dementiev
Printer: Toppan Leefung Printing Ltd

10 9 8 7 6 5 4 3 2

Keep up with New Holland Publishers on Facebook
www.facebook.com/NewHollandPublishers

Backyard Bird Sounds

FRED VAN GESSEL

CONTENTS

Introduction 6

TRACK NO.	SPECIES	PAGE NO.
01.	Black Swan	8
02.	Australian Wood Duck	9
03.	Pacific Black Duck	9
04.	Spotted Dove	10
05.	Crested Pigeon	10
06.	Tawny Frogmouth	11
07.	White-faced Heron	12
08.	Collared Sparrowhawk	12
09.	Nankeen Kestrel	13
10.	Peregrine Falcon	13
11.	Masked Lapwing	14
12.	Silver Gull	15
13.	Yellow-tailed Black-cockatoo	16
14.	Galah	17
15.	Little Corella	17
16.	Sulphur-crested Cockatoo	18
17.	Rainbow Lorikeet	19
18.	Crimson Rosella	20
19.	Pheasant Coucal	21
20.	Eastern Koel	21

TRACK NO.	SPECIES	PAGE NO.
21.	Channel-billed Cuckoo	22
22.	Shining Bronze-cuckoo	23
23.	Fan-tailed Cuckoo	23
24.	Powerful Owl	24
25.	Southern Boobook	25
26.	Eastern Barn Owl	25
27.	Laughing Kookaburra	26
28.	Blue-winged Kookaburra	27
29.	Sacred Kingfisher	27
30.	Dollarbird	28
31.	Satin Bowerbird	29
32.	Great Bowerbird	30
33.	Superb Fairy-wren	31
34.	Variegated Fairy-wren	32
35.	White-browed Scrubwren	32
36.	Yellow-rumped Thornbill	33
37.	Brown Thornbill	33
38.	Spotted Pardalote	34
39.	Striated Pardalote	35
40.	Eastern Spinebill	36

TRACK NO.	SPECIES	PAGE NO.
41.	Western Spinebill	36
42.	Lewin's Honeyeater	37
43.	Singing Honeyeater	37
44.	Yellow-faced Honeyeater	38
45.	White-plumed Honeyeater	38
46.	Noisy Miner	39
47.	Little Wattlebird	40
48.	Red Wattlebird	41
49.	Brown Honeyeater	41
50.	New Holland Honeyeater	42
51.	Noisy Friarbird	43
52.	Blue-faced Honeyeater	43
53.	Black-faced Cuckoo-shrike	44
54.	White-bellied Cuckoo-shrike	44
55.	Grey Shrike-thrush	45
56.	Green Figbird	45
57.	Yellow Oriole	46
58.	Olive-backed Oriole	46
59.	Black Butcherbird	47
60.	Grey Butcherbird	47

TRACK NO.	SPECIES	PAGE NO.
61.	Pied Butcherbird	48
62.	Australian Magpie	49
63.	Spangled Drongo	50
64.	Pied Currawong	50
65.	Grey Fantail	51
66.	Willie Wagtail	52
67.	Australian Raven	53
68.	Torresian Crow	53
69.	Magpielark	54
70.	Silvereye	55
71.	Welcome Swallow	56
72.	Fairy Martin	57
73.	Tree Martin	57
74.	Mistletoebird	58

Image Credits	58
Track Listing	59
Bibliography	62
Index	64

INTRODUCTION

In many overseas countries interest in birds and birdwatching as a study of natural history, and as a form of recreation, has been accepted for many decades. In Australia the study of birds and bird song has been comparatively slow, but the involvement of many amateur birdwatchers has greatly increased knowledge of our birdlife and has now become a common and enjoyable hobby.

This book and accompanying CD has been produced with the intention of gaining interest through people identifying and studying some of Australia's more common garden birds. Approximately 750 species of birds occur in Australia on a regular basis and another 85 vagrants have also been recorded. Of these about 20 per cent or 150 species regularly occur in urban areas and are frequently found in towns and city gardens.

Australia has many distinctive birds, some are easily seen and heard, but their appearances and sounds may vary from region to region from the northern to the southern coastal districts, from the east coast to the west coast and in inland regions.

This book attempts to assist in the identification of some of the more common birds likely to be seen in your garden through giving a photographic image, a description, and most of all by their calls and songs.

Many birds are often heard but not seen and knowing their calls and their songs will help enormously in making a correct identification. I have tried to incorporate as many sounds commonly uttered by the species, but it must be appreciated that these represent only a fraction of all sounds produced. To make the identification by sound alone a little more difficult, birds of a particular species widely distributed in many parts of the country may make different calls, called 'geographical variation,' which is sometimes noticeable even within very short distances. Most birds make a variety of calls throughout the season, some may only be heard at a particular time of the year, some may only sing during the early morning, while others may only sing their courtship song during the breeding season until they have found a suitable partner. Song has an important biological function and is vital to the survival of the species. It is a basic part of the ritual of territory selection, courtship, display and mating. Many birds in Australia are also accomplished mimics and ventriloquists and when listening to their song one should not jump to immediate conclusions… instead it is best to listen for some time.

It is hoped that this book will help in the identification of birds found in your garden.

FRED VAN GESSEL

01 | Black Swan
Cygnus atratus

The Black Swan is a widespread and common bird throughout most of Australia including Tasmania. It was introduced to New Zealand between 1864 and 1868, and is now common on the North and South Islands. Birds are usually found in pairs, small family parties or in very large flocks, sometimes numbering thousands at certain times of the year. In drought years few birds attempt to breed and will seek wetter areas until the drought breaks, when they return and commence nesting almost immediately. Like all waterfowl Black Swans moult all their flight feathers at once and temporarily become flightless for a period of about four weeks. During that period birds seek safety in dense vegetation or on large open water bodies, keeping far out from the shore. They are primarily herbivorous, feeding on aquatic plants, but they also take aquatic insects, crustaceans, and sometimes small fish. Feeds by surface-feeding or by up-ending in deeper waters.

RANGE AND HABITAT: Found throughout Australia on lakes, swamps and marshes, shallow estuaries, large salt lakes, coastal lagoons, saltpans and salt marshes, mudflats and flooded or irrigated temporary pasture lands.

BREEDING: Breeds in fresh, brackish or saline, but not tidal, wetlands with enough soft vegetation to build the nest, feed the young and shelter in tall vegetation. They breed seasonally throughout the year when conditions are suitable. The nest is a considerable platform, often used for many years, consisting of reeds, grasses and other plant material in shallow water, lined with down where 4-6 greenish-white eggs are laid and incubated by the female alone, while the male remains nearby.

TRACK NO. 01: The voice is a musical bugle or trumpeting given in flight or when socialising in a group.

02 | Australian Wood Duck
Chenonetta jubata

Sedentary and highly terrestrial; often seen grazing on land. Has characteristic shape and posture with long legs and extended neck, reflected in its alternative name, 'Maned Goose.'

Adult male vermiculated grey, with brown head and black rump, tail and undertail-coverts. Female has a pale brown head with two pale stripes and a coarsely speckled breast.

RANGE AND HABITAT: Widespread in wetter places, on open pastures, lightly timbered country near water, farm dams, parks and gardens, golf courses, and where ever there is short grass or herbage.

BREEDING: September to November in the south and January to March in northern New South Wales and southern Queensland or at any time after good rainfall or flooding. Nests in hollow trees (sometimes far from water) and lays 7–12 creamy-white eggs. After breeding gathers in flocks.

TRACK NO. 02: The male's highly distinctive, cat-like *wee-ou* is often uttered by lone birds or in flight. The female's call is a loud, hoarse *whoo*.

03 | Pacific Black Duck
Anas superciliosa

Abundant and widespread dabbling duck. Mainly sedentary. Can become tame when living in close proximity to human settlement. Sexes similar. Up-ends in shallows to search for submerged or emergent floating vegetation and aquatic invertebrates. Beware of hybrids with the introduced Mallard, *A. platyrhynchos*.

RANGE AND HABITAT: Found in fresh and salt water over much of the continent. Very common in coastal districts and along most big rivers, particularly the Murray-Darling basin. In times of inland floods can be found over much of the arid interior.

BREEDING: In the south usually breeds in spring after good winter rainfall (July to October), but in northern Australia breeds after the wet season. Inland breeds after heavy rains and during floods. Will nest almost anywhere, but most frequently in stumps, tree hollows or in thick vegetation on the ground.

TRACK NO. 03: Quick persistent quacks and single drawn out quacks; high-pitched whistle call followed by deep resonant grunt.

04 | **Spotted Dove**
Streptopelia chinensis

Native to Asia, this species was introduced in various Australian cities between 1870–1940. Plumage grey-brown with white-spotted black collar and broad white terminal tail-band. In courtship display rises high into the air, then glides down slowly.

Feeds on ground, taking seeds, weeds, grain, wheat and scraps discarded by people.

RANGE AND HABITAT: Common resident in most cities and towns, frequenting parks and gardens. Also inhabits rural areas close to large settlements, often near grain silos.

BREEDING: Generally breeds throughout year on east coast; in Victoria, main breeding period is September to November; in south-west Western Australia breeds in spring and summer. Nest is a flimsy platform of sticks and twigs placed in trees, bushes and buildings. May have two or three broods in one season.

TRACK NO. 04: The advertising call varies as *coo, coo-croo, coo-coo croo,* or *coo-coo-oo-krook* varying from one to four notes. Other calls are a two-syllable *coo, croo.*

05 | **Crested Pigeon**
Ocyphaps lophotes

Usually seen in pairs or small flocks, occasionally in larger flocks. Often found not far from water and regularly comes to drink during the first hour after sunrise and around dusk.

Swift flight consists of several rapid wing-beats alternating with gliding on horizontally extended wings.

Wings whistle on take-off; on landing, tail is flicked high above body. Feeds primarily on seeds and other plant material; also takes insects and small animals.

RANGE AND HABITAT: Common throughout Australia in most coastal and agricultural districts, parks and suburbs. Not found in rainforests.

BREEDING: Breeds at all seasons but near the southern coastal regions is a spring and summer breeder. Nest is an untidy, frail, flat platform of interlocking twigs, usually placed in a bush or tree. Fledglings are fed for a few days on 'milk' from the parents' crops.

TRACK NO. 05: Utters soft plaintive *coo* or *whoo-oo* but in courtship the call is often preceded with a bill snap, sounding like a click before the *whoo*.

06 | Tawny Frogmouth
Podargus strigoides

The Tawny Frogmouth is a common bird, familiar to many people in Australia. They are generally sedentary, long-lived birds which pair for life. Perhaps because of their nocturnal habits they are often confused with owls; although the only thing they have in common is that they have big eyes, soft plumage for silent flight and hunt by night.

To avoid being harassed by other birds, frogmouths spend most of the day roosting motionless in a tree, camouflaged as a dead branch. They roost singly, in pairs or in small groups close to one another. When disturbed or discovered during the day, roosting birds are often mobbed by other species of birds. At night they often sit on fence posts or other perches as they search for insects or other food. After locating their prey they silently glide down or pounce and snap up their victim. They feed on a variety of foods but their main diet consists of insects, such as beetles, crickets and moths, while they also take worms, lizards, frogs, small snakes, small birds and small rodents.

RANGE AND HABITAT: Found in open woodland, parks and gardens throughout Australia and Tasmania, except for far western Queensland, central Northern Territory, and the open plains and treeless deserts. They tend to avoid rainforest.

BREEDING: The nest is a flimsy and frail untidy platform of twigs and sticks usually placed on a horizontal fork or branch where two or sometimes three eggs are laid. The breeding season usually occurs from August to November but in the dry inland regions often starts after rains.

TRACK NO. 06: They produce a series of *ooom* calls of low intensity, hoots of various frequencies, screams, purring, screeching and hissing.

07 | White-faced Heron
Egretta novaehollandiae

This bluish-grey heron with yellowish-green feet is named after its conspicuous white face and throat.

It often feeds along the edges of a creek, on coastal mudflats, in wet grass or in swamps. Birds stir the muddy water and weeds with their feet to obtain the creatures that are disturbed. They feed on a variety of aquatic and terrestrial insects, frogs, fish, lizards and sometimes small birds.

RANGE AND HABITAT: The most common and widespread resident heron in Australia. Found all around the coast and on inland waterways.

BREEDING: The breeding season is usually from August to January but is influenced by seasonal weather conditions. Often nests in trees close to water, building a rather frail structure from sticks and twigs. Both parents incubate the 3–6 bluish-green eggs which take up to four weeks to hatch. The young remain in the nest for a further 5–6 weeks.

TRACK NO. 07: Croaks, usually in flight or when alarmed.

08 | Collared Sparrowhawk
Accipiter cirrocephalus

Flight is swift with quick wing-beats interspersed with long fast glides and often seen soaring and circling in the sky. Has short rounded wings and a long tail, so that it can fly through forests with great speed and agility while hunting. Prey consists of small birds, mammals and lizards and sometimes flying insects. The sexes differ greatly in size, the male being much smaller and weighing half as much.

RANGE AND HABITAT: Widespread in many types of forest and grassland, also in wooded areas of farmland and urban areas.

BREEDING: Breeding season from July to February. While the female is incubating the male hunts and brings food, which he passes to her in the air.

TRACK NO. 08: Several main calls are recognised such as rapid chittering, soft mewing and slow chatter. Call is a fast and loud repeated *swee-swee-swee* or *sweep-sweep sweep*, rapid chittering *ki-ki-ki-ki-ki-ki* at about six syllables, also *kek-kek-kek-kek* and rapid shrill chatter *e-e-e-e*.

09 | Nankeen Kestrel
Falco cenchroides

These long-winged reddish-brown falcons are often seen sitting on telegraph- or fence-posts, or hovering in search of small animals, birds and insects. The name 'Nankeen,' referring to the colour of the birds, is actually derived from the colours of a cotton cloth manufactured in the Chinese town of Nanjing.

RANGE AND HABITAT: Widespread and common. Occurs in most habitats from open woodland to savanna, cultivated lands and urban environments. Some populations move in response to local abundances of food, such as rodent plagues.

BREEDING: Breeds throughout Australia, often in tree hollows or old nests of other birds, in crevices on cliffs, in buildings or even abandoned cars. The clutch size is usually 3–5 speckled brown eggs and laying occurs from July to December. The male provides most of the female's food during the four-week incubation period.

TRACK NO. 09: Calls are described as chatters, twitters, screams, trills, whines, ticking and clucking. A high-pitched chattering *kee-kee kee* or *kik-kik-kik* is most commonly heard.

10 | Peregrine Falcon
Falco peregrinus

The Peregrine has the widest breeding distribution of any bird species in the world. It is the epitome of a raptor that hunts by speed, taking birds in flight. Favoured prey includes pigeons, waterfowl and shorebirds, although many other species are taken. In recent years Peregrines have moved into city centres and started to nest on tall buildings.

RANGE AND HABITAT: Sedentary and inhabits inland tree-lined watercourses, woodland, pastures, swamps, eucalypt forest, offshore islands and cities throughout Australia.

BREEDING: Nesting season is generally from June to November, but in the north from April to June. Nests in a shallow scrape on a ledge, in an abandoned nest of another large bird, or in a tall hollow tree. Female does most of the incubation, which starts with the second egg and lasts about 33 days. The young leave the nest at about six weeks.

TRACK NO. 10: Female begging call is a plaintive, nasal *wheeee-wheee*. Young birds in the nest have a piercing scream.

11 | Masked Lapwing
Vanellus miles

The Masked Lapwing, formerly known as the 'Spur-winged Plover,' was so aptly named because of the large yellow spur on the 'shoulder' of its wings. It is a large and conspicuous shorebird which is very aggressive when nesting, often chasing and calling loudly while dive-bombing the intruder.

It is a mainly brown-and-white shorebird with long legs, a black crown, a black stripe extending down the neck and sides of the upper breast, and a yellow bill and yellow facial wattles. These birds are sometimes very noisy when interactions occur, with much upright posturing, especially during the breeding season and when flocks form during autumn and winter.

They forage in wet pasture, grassland, golf courses, mud- and sand-flats, estuaries and seashores, where they feed on a variety of insects, crustaceans, molluscs, worms and occasionally seeds and some herbaceous plants. While feeding along the shoreline the birds often stir the muddy water with their feet to obtain the creatures that are flushed. Also uses foot-tapping to find food while on grass.

RANGE AND HABITAT: Favours a wide range of natural and modified habitats. Widespread and common in all parts of Australia, except in Western Australia where it mainly occurs in the north. Also found on Norfolk Island, Lord Howe Island and in New Zealand.

BREEDING: In the north they breed at almost any time of year if conditions are favourable, in the south mainly between May and July. They lay 2–4 eggs on the ground, in a shallow depression lined with grass, but can also be found nesting on flat rooftops, in parks and football ovals or near roadsides. The young leave the nest as soon as they are hatched.

TRACK NO. 11: Very noisy and often calls at night. A repeated staccato *keer-ki-ki-ki-ki* or *krik-krik-krik* or a sharp *kek*.

12 | Silver Gull
Chroicocephalus novaehollandiae

A grey-and-white gull with boldly patterned black-and-white wing-tips. Adults have a red bill and red legs and feet. The eye-ring can be silver or red depending on sex and age. In their first year young Silver Gulls are a mottled brown above with brownish eyes, legs and bill, gradually changing colour over a couple of years until they attain adult plumage.

This species has adapted well to humans and over the past 40 years its numbers have increased dramatically. The Silver Gull steals the eggs and young of other ground-nesting birds, often eliminating entire clutches of rare species. Inland they are often seen feeding in open paddocks, looking for worms or insects. They also feed on small fish, crustaceans and other sea-creatures they can catch and also are often seen scavenging behind fishing boats. In Melbourne and Sydney they scavenge for food scraps and hundreds commute daily for this purpose.

RANGE AND HABITAT: The most common and widespread gull in Australia. Coastal, frequenting seashores and offshore islands, but also inland lakes and swamps.

BREEDING: The timing of the breeding season is variable throughout Australia. Birds nest colonially in a variety of situations, including on offshore islands, coastal or inland and on artificial constructions and flat roofs. In Sydney Harbour they even nest on boats left unattended for some time. They have adapted to inland conditions and nest on exposed spits of sand or shingle. In some areas in Western Australia they have two breeding seasons. Some of the larger colonies are now near cities because most urban areas have rubbish tips on which the gulls forage.

TRACK NO. 12: The common call is a drawn-out *kaarr.* Young birds have a peevish call often given in a submissive posture towards adults.

13 | Yellow-tailed Black-cockatoo
Calyptorhynchus funereus

The Yellow-tailed Black-cockatoo is a large brownish-black cockatoo with a yellow cheek-patch and a long, slightly rounded tail. The tail has a broad yellow band across the centre which can be spotted brownish-black. This is a conspicuous species which usually occurs in small groups, although occasionally large flocks can congregate, especially in pine plantations. These birds have long, broad wings, a slow-flapping buoyant flight, and often call in flight. Historically the species was known as the 'Funereal Cockatoo.'

Birds forage in a wide variety of habitats, including pine forests, orchards and coastal heathlands, and feed on a large variety of foods, such as seeds, nuts, berries, fruits, blossom and insects. This species is unique among cockatoos in that invertebrates sometimes dominate its diet. Its bill is adapted for gouging out wood and for the extraction of wood-boring larvae of insects. Extraction of insect larvae from tree trunks causes damage that leads to the collapse and destruction of trees, particularly saplings. Because of these destructive feeding habits the birds are sometimes considered pests in orchards and forestry and eucalyptus plantations.

RANGE AND HABITAT: Common and widespread throughout the south-east and east coast of Australia to about 23°S. They are mainly birds of the tall wet coastal and mountain forests and coastal woodlands dominated by Banksia with an understorey of *Hakea*.

BREEDING: Breeding season is variable and is restricted to areas where there are large trees. In northern New South Wales and Queensland the breeding season lasts from March to August, while in south-eastern South Australia and Victoria it runs from November to February, sometimes later.

TRACK NO. 13: The calls are a loud *kee-ah*, *kee-ah* repeated several times, and chuckling and giggling noises usually given in flight. They also utter grating, grinding and begging noises while feeding.

14 | Galah
Eolophus roseicapillus

This pink-and-grey parrot is generally sedentary although young birds may disperse widely. In winter large flocks, sometimes numbering in the hundreds, can be seen feeding in fields foraging for seeds, fruits and insects. Much of a Galah's day is spent sitting in a tree waiting for digestion to make room for the next meal.

RANGE AND HABITAT: Common throughout most of Australia in savanna woodlands. Absent from extreme north-eastern coastal rainforests, south-west Western Australia and Tasmania. Has colonised open country of all types, including suburban gardens and parks. Inland found in eucalypt woodland and along watercourses.

BREEDING: In the temperate regions breeds in spring (August to December), in tropical areas during the dry winter months (February to June), but in dry inland areas breeding occurs in any month depending on rainfall. Pairs form long-lasting bonds and may nest in the same tree hollow for many years.

TRACK NO. 14: A variety of whistling notes and harsh screeching territorial calls; single- and double-syllable high-pitched screams, often in flight.

15 | Little Corella
Cacatua sanguinea

Medium-sized crestless white cockatoo with a large patch of bare blue skin around eye. Feeds primarily on ground on seeds, legumes, roots and bulbs and, particularly on the eastern coasts, often seen feeding in flocks in parkland where they dig up onion weed bulbs.

During periods of drought and food shortage flocks of thousands can congregate in agricultural areas to feed on grain and grass seeds.

RANGE AND HABITAT: Widespread and common in arid and semi-arid areas and parts of the south-east and north. Found in a variety of habitats, including open woodland, scrub and grassland. Often most common around tree-lined watercourses.

BREEDING: Favoured nest-site is in a hollow river gum; seldom breeds far from water. Breeding season variable: June to October on the east coast, February to May in the north. Pairs are site-faithful and use a nest hollow for many years.

TRACK NO. 15: Utters a range of raucous calls and screeches. Silent and very secretive while breeding.

16 | Sulphur-crested Cockatoo
Cacatua galerita

A large white cockatoo with a distinctive long yellow crest and pale yellow ear-patch. The species is common and is one of the most easily recognised cockatoos in Australia. Considerable variation in size occurs in different parts of the range. Sulphur-crested Cockatoos are long-lived and are also one of the most popular aviary birds. Over the past 50 years, aviary releases have resulted in the establishment of feral populations in south-west Western Australia.

Their food consist of nuts, seeds of grasses and thistles, roots, berries, herbaceous plants and insects and their larvae. They can become a pest, causing damage to crops. In towns and urban areas where people tend to feed these birds they can become very destructive. Chewing by cockatoos can cause significant damage to buildings, particularly the soft decorative timbers, cabling, television aerials and satellite dishes. Large flocks of cockatoos can also generate sufficient noise to cause a nuisance when they are coming and going to their roosting sites, particularly during the late evening and morning.

RANGE AND HABITAT: Common throughout its range, which extends from the tropical north to the temperate eastern and south-eastern coast of Australia and Tasmania. Generally absent from arid and semi-arid regions. They frequent a wide variety of habitats including farmlands, open pasture, sclerophyll forests, savanna woodland and adjoining riverside vegetation.

BREEDING: Breeding season variable. In the south it runs from August to January and in the north from May to September. During that time birds are usually found in pairs and are very wary and difficult to approach. Tall trees with hollow limbs near riverbanks and creeks are their favourite nesting places.

TRACK NO. 16: An extremely noisy bird when in flocks, with a wide variety of raucous screeching and squawks.

17 | Rainbow Lorikeet
Tricoglossus haematodus

Rainbow Lorikeets are beautiful birds, displaying all the colours of the spectrum in their plumage. They are particularly prolific in coastal Queensland and northern New South Wales, and they are common in both urban and rural districts. There are two different forms in Australia, the subspecies *rubitorquis* (which is 'split' by some authorities as a separate species, the Red-collared Lorikeet, *T. rubitorquis*) is found mainly found in the tropical north and north-west and the subspecies *novaehollandiae* occurs along the east and south-east coasts of Australia.

These parrots are active and very noisy, especially when feeding on the blossom of native trees where they are attracted to the nectar and pollen. They have a retractile brushy-tipped tongue which is well adapted for gathering pollen and nectar. They also eat seeds, fruits, berries and insects. Rainbow Lorikeets have adapted well to human environments and can often be seen and heard in suburban backyards where they can become quite tame. The Currumbin Sanctuary on the Gold Coast of Queensland has become a famous tourist attraction for viewing the daily feeding sessions of hundreds of these birds. They are very sociable and congregate in very large and noisy flocks after breeding and when roosting communally.

RANGE AND HABITAT: Inhabits a wide variety of forested habitats of the northern parts of the Northern Territory, eastern Australia, throughout Victoria and in south-eastern South Australia and on Kangaroo Island, but is a rare visitor to Tasmania.

BREEDING: Breeds mainly in the spring and summer months, but breeding also takes place at other times of year when suitable conditions occur. Usually nests in hollow limbs or trunks of trees, but also in palms. The male is often seen at or near the entrance to the hollow when the female is brooding.

TRACK NO. 17: In flight utters screeching contact calls repeatedly. When feeding gives a soft twittering and shrill chattering.

18 | Crimson Rosella
Platycercus elegans

The rosellas are some of the most colourful parrots in Australia; all species having distinctive coloured cheek patches. The Crimson Rosella, also called 'Mountain Lowry,' is one of the best-known and most familiar species of the rosella group and it is a popular aviary bird. It is well known from the eastern states of Australia where three colour forms occur in the coastal forests and mountain regions from Queensland down to the Adelaide hills. The Crimson form, with its red-and-blue plumage, is found from Brisbane south to Melbourne. A mottled orange form, known as the 'Adelaide Rosella,' is found in the Adelaide hills, and a yellow-and-blue form, known as the 'Yellow Rosella,' is found in the Murray Valley. All three forms have a red forehead and blue tail, wings and cheek patch.

These rosellas are mainly sedentary, but some populations may be nomadic. They all feed on seeds of acacias, eucalypts and a wide range of native and introduced trees, as well as fruits, berries, nuts, blossom, nectar and insects.

RANGE AND HABITAT: A bird of humid to semi-humid forests, found from sea-level up to the highest mountains throughout its range. It is common to abundant, occurring in well-established suburban gardens in the major cities such as Sydney, Canberra and Melbourne. In north-eastern and south-eastern Queensland it is confined to highland forest, but further south it is found in rainforests, sclerophyll forest, coastal heathland, orchards, urban parks and gardens. Also occurs on Kangaroo Island, South Australia.

BREEDING: The breeding season runs from early September to January and they nest in a hollow limb or hole in a tree.

TRACK NO. 18: Contact call is a disyllabic *cusick-cusick*; lots of piping notes resembling *kwik-kweek-kwik* or *kwik-kweek*; alarm call is a series of shrill shrieks.

19 | Pheasant Coucal
Centropus phasianinus

This sturdy, long-tailed bird lives mainly on the ground. It is the only Australian bird in the cuckoo family that builds its own nest and incubates and rears its own young.

Back, wings and tail barred rufous. Head and underparts black during breeding and straw-coloured in non-breeding plumage. Sexes similar but female larger.

Feeds on ground on a variety of invertebrates and small animals. When disturbed flies clumsily for a short distance, but generally reluctant to fly far.

RANGE AND HABITAT: Sedentary. Common in wetter areas along the north and east coasts. Found in open forest with dense undergrowth, sugar cane fields and swampy areas.

BREEDING: Nests from September to May. A dome-shaped nest is usually placed in thick vegetation.

TRACK NO. 19: A series of *hoop-hoo-hoop* calls, initially slow then faster and slows again at the end. Alarm calls *nah-oo*, *nah-oo* or sharp *tschew* or scolding *chew*. Male call is higher-pitched than female and pairs often duet.

20 | Eastern Koel
Eudynamys orientalis

Male distinctive glossy black with a red iris and stout whitish bill. Female blackish-brown above with bold white spotting and barring.

Known colloquially as 'rainbird,' its summer arrival from New Guinea and the Solomon Islands usually coincides with the wet season. The male, on its return, destroys the nests of birds such as wattlebirds and orioles to ensure an ample supply of nests in which the female koel can deposit her eggs.

Feeds on insects, small animals and fruits. Often found in suburban gardens, parks or streets with fruit-bearing trees such as mangoes and figs.

RANGE AND HABITAT: Occupies a wide range of woodland habitats. Range confined to wetter areas on the north and east coasts of Australia south to Victoria.

BREEDING: A migratory brood-parasite, breeding in the austral summer from October to December.

TRACK NO. 20: Repeated and far-carrying *coo-ee* or *kooell*, also *wurroo-wurroo*; rapid shrill screeches *keek-keek-keek-keek*. Their incessant calling can be quite annoying to some people.

21 | Channel-billed Cuckoo
Scythrops novaehollandiae

The largest parasitic cuckoo in the world. A very large and distinctive pale grey bird with a huge hornbill-like bill. In flight shows long pointed wings and a long narrow tail. The Channel-billed is a migratory cuckoo whose arrival in Australia to breed in early September coincides with the onset of the wet season in the north. They herald their arrival with raucous calling and are often mobbed by magpies, currawongs or kookaburras. The birds return to their wintering grounds in Indonesia and Papua New Guinea between early January and March.

On their breeding grounds they occur solitarily or in pairs, but during migration become very gregarious and often feed and roost communally in large fig trees. They feed on fruits, particularly native figs, berries and insects, and are not averse of taking small birds.

RANGE AND HABITAT: Occurs in a wide variety of habitats, including monsoon and eucalypt forest, woodland, wet sclerophyll forest, rainforest with abundant fruit trees, farm woodland, gardens with fruit trees and orchards. The range extends from the Kimberleys in Western Australia to the Northern Territory, and from coastal northern Queensland and New South Wales, where they are widespread, down to Victoria. It is a scarce bird in the inland parts of Australia.

BREEDING: Breeds in sub-coastal north and east Australia from October to January, parasitising some of the bigger host birds such as crows and ravens, Australian Magpie, butcherbirds, Magpielark, currawongs and sometimes even hawks and falcons.

TRACK NO. 21: Usually in flight gives a loud, raucous, far-carrying *waack-waack-waack* repeated several times. When perched often utters *ko-ko-ko-ko-ko*, and when mobbed gives a harsh croak. The fledglings utter similar calls to young Pied Currawongs.

22 | Shining Bronze-cuckoo
Chrysococcyx lucidus

A small cuckoo usually seen singly or in pairs. Distinguished from other bronze-cuckoos by the diagnostic combination of bronze cap and mantle, blackish eye and white belly with bold and complete dark barring.

Gleans invertebrates and their larvae from the foliage of trees and shrubs.

RANGE AND HABITAT: Widespread in rainforest, woodland, heathland, mangroves, parks and gardens from the coastal regions in south-west Western Australia and all along the east coast. Birds from south-east Australia winter in Queensland and Papua New Guinea, those from south-west Western Australia winter in the Lesser Sundas. The New Zealand race, *lucidus*, migrates to the Solomon Islands via the east coast of Australia.

BREEDING: Breeds from October to April in southern parts of Australia. Parasitises the nests of small birds, especially warblers, fairy-wrens, scrubwrens and thornbills.

TRACK NO. 22: Calls mostly during spring and summer from a high perch in the canopy. Four to five clear descending notes like a dog whistle *fwee-fwee-fwee-fwee-fweer*, also a trilling sound and a staccato *pee-eeerr*.

23 | Fan-tailed Cuckoo
Cacomantis flabeliformis

A medium-sized blue-grey cuckoo with a rufous breast. Tail longish with bold white edges and often fanned. In flight resembles a hawk and perhaps because of this often mobbed by small birds. Feeds on a variety of invertebrates, but preferred prey is hairy caterpillars. Usually found singly or in pairs.

RANGE AND HABITAT: Fairly common throughout range. Breeds all along the south and east coasts of Australia, including in Tasmania. Found in a variety of habitats, including tropical, sub-tropical and temperate rainforest, wet sclerophyll forest, woodland, heathland, scrubland, parks and gardens. In south present from early September to late April, in north some populations are partly migratory, nomadic or sedentary.

BREEDING: Breeding season mostly from August to December, but some sedentary populations may breed at other times of the year. Parasitises nests of small birds such as thornbills, scrubwrens, gerygones, mistletoebirds and fairy-wrens.

TRACK NO. 23: Often calls at night. Calls include a slow descending trill *peeeer*, a high-pitched *chireee* and a monotonous whistle *foofeee*.

24 | Powerful Owl
Ninox strenua

The Powerful Owl is the largest Australian owl. Its range is restricted to south-eastern Australia. Males are considerably bigger than females, with broader heads and flatter crowns. Juveniles are generally smaller and whiter than adults, and often with a considerable amount of down.

Diet consists mainly of arboreal mammals, such as possums and gliders, birds and flying foxes taken at night. They also prey on smaller animals such as rats and bandicoots, and sometimes large insects. Like some of the other Australian owls, the Powerful Owl can often be seen roosting in a shady spot throughout the day, holding with one foot the partly eaten remains of a possum, squirrel or flying fox.

A pair of Powerful Owls may occupy a territory of several square kilometres and their presence is often indicated by patches of chalky white excreta below a roosting or nesting tree.

RANGE AND HABITAT: Found throughout south-eastern Australia and north to south-east Queensland. Its favourite habitats are wet and hilly, heavily timbered forests with dense gullies adjacent to more open woodland. Sometimes occurs in parks and gardens.

BREEDING: The breeding season runs from about April to early July. The female lays two white eggs, which she alone incubates for approximately 38 days. The young leave the nest in about September but they stay with their parents for three or four months after leaving the nest site.

TRACK NO. 24: The usual call of the owl is a deep-throated and far-carrying *whoo-hoo*, with the female's being slightly higher in pitch. Sometimes a single *whoo* is also uttered, particularly when aggressive; other calls are strange tremulous bleating and the juveniles utter a chirruping trill.

25 | Southern Boobook
Ninox novaehollandiae

Australia's most common owl. Small to medium in size with a spectacled appearance and pale yellow eyes. Also known as the 'Mopoke,' which can be rather confusing as this colloquial name is shared with the unrelated Tawny Frogmouth. Diet includes of all kinds of insects, worms, small reptiles and birds, rats and mice.

RANGE AND HABITAT: Common throughout Australia in a wide range of habitats including open woodland, orchards, gardens and city parks.

BREEDING: Breeds from about August to April, usually in a hollow tree or rock cavity. Lays two or three rounded white eggs. Often uses same site year after year. Eggs brooded almost exclusively by female.

TRACK NO. 25: Common call a distinctive double '*boo book*' or '*mo poke*' repeated many times, but also makes a frog-like purring '*por-por-por*' which can last for several minutes Also a cat like mew '*ow-ow-ow*' and a *yowl* call. Young birds make a trill similar to a stridulating insect.

26 | Eastern Barn Owl
Tyto javanica

Very pale with a heart-shaped face. A specialist hunter mainly of small ground mammals. Uses hearing to locate prey in almost total darkness. Barn owls have undoubtedly been at the root of some ghostly stories, and one tale is that their bioluminescent feathers have been reported as the 'min min lights' in outback Australia.

The Australian race *delicatula* is 'split' by some authorities as a separate species: Australian Barn Owl, *Tyto delicatula*.

RANGE AND HABITAT: Widespread and common in open woodland and farmland over most of Australia, but rare in Tasmania. Also occurs in parks and gardens in suburbia. Young birds disperse widely.

BREEDING: An opportunistic breeder and may breed at any time of the year when a continuous food supply is available. In times of rodent plagues will breed several times in the season.

TRACK NO. 26: Males utter harsh hissing screeches when in flight or in territorial displays. Courting birds make a variety of chirruping, chattering and wheezing calls and young in the nest give rasping calls when begging for food.

27 | Laughing Kookaburra
Dacelo novaeguineae

Few native species have adapted to city and suburban life as well as the Laughing Kookaburra, also called 'Laughing Jackass,' which is the largest of the kingfisher family.

Laughing Kookaburras are sedentary and long-lived birds that remain faithful to the same location for many years, living in a hierarchical family group consisting of a dominant breeding pair and their adult offspring from previous mating, which help with feeding the next brood. Only with the aid of helpers are they able to raise a full brood. The reason seems to be the difficulty in finding enough food in the dry Australian forests.

They feed on invertebrates, worms, small frogs, reptiles, rodents and birds, and will sometimes also catch small fish by plunge-diving. They have superb vision and often sit on a favourite perch watching and waiting for movement some distance away and then swooping with a gliding dive to capture prey. They usually return to the same perch and then use their bill to beat the prey on a branch.

RANGE AND HABITAT: Found in open dry eucalypt forest, open woodland, farmland, along watercourses and in city parks and gardens in the eastern and southern states of Australia. They have also been successfully introduced and are now well established in Western Australia, Tasmania and New Zealand.

BREEDING: Nests in tree hollows or termite nests in trees from September to December, sometimes earlier. Lays a clutch of 2–4 eggs, which are incubated by both parents and previous years' offspring which act as helpers.

TRACK NO. 27: The famous laugh is the territorial song, mainly given at dawn and dusk, which is usually uttered by two or more birds. They also make raucous calls when chasing or attacking intruders such as Lace Monitors.

28 | Blue-winged Kookaburra
Dacelo leachii

Easily confused with Laughing Kookaburra, but smaller with a pale eye, dark brown back, white ear-coverts and large areas of pale blue in wings and rump. Also has distinctive voice. Male has bright blue tail and female's is rufous with dark blue bars. Diet and nesting preferences are very similar to those of Laughing.

RANGE AND HABITAT: Wooded savannas from the Kimberleys in Western Australia across the Northern Territory and to south-eastern Queensland.

BREEDING: Breeds from September to January. Nests in ground termitaria and in tree holes, laying 2–5 eggs. Lives in a hierarchical family group consisting of a dominant breeding pair and their adult offspring.

TRACK NO. 28: Territorial song given by two or three birds in unison and sounds like a maniacal and far-carrying screeching cackle, *kuk-kuk-kuk-kuk*. Also soft growls and loud hooting barks ending abruptly in a wild *ow-ow-ow*. In a duet one bird usually calls at a higher pitch. Particularly vocal during dawn and dusk.

29 | Sacred Kingfisher
Todiramphus sanctus

Australia's most familiar small land kingfisher. Upperparts bluish-green with a black band from bill around the nape and a buff spot in front of eye. Underparts buff to white. Often sits patiently on a branch, powerline or other perch and glides to snatch prey from ground or plunge-dives into shallow water. Diet mainly consists of a variety of invertebrates, but also lizards, crabs and occasionally small fish.

RANGE AND HABITAT: Widely distributed in Australia, resident in the north and migratory in the south. Populations from the latter migrate to the Solomon Islands, Indonesia and New Guinea, returning to Australia from late August. Common in all types of open woodland, river margins, farmland, lakes and coastal habitats.

BREEDING: Breeds from September to March. Nests in an earthen bank, tree hollow or termite nest high in a tree.

TRACK NO. 29: Utters a repeated loud *kek-kek-kek* or *keek-keek-keek-keek* during the breeding season but otherwise noticeably silent.

30 | Dollarbird
Eurystomus orientalis

The Dollarbird or 'Dollar Roller' is a stout, short-tailed greenish bird with a large rounded brownish head, glossy blue throat, short broad red bill and red legs. In flight it shows a prominent pale whitish wing-patch on long broad wings, also referred to as a 'dollar-mark'; hence the name Dollarbird. It is very acrobatic in flight, tumbling and turning, diving and rolling rapidly from side to side interspersed with glides.

This is a summer-breeding migratory bird which arrives in Australia from September and leaves again between February–May to spend the winter in New Guinea, the Bismarck Archipelago and Indonesia. The birds are noisy and conspicuous after arriving at their breeding site, particularly during courtship flights and when chasing intruders. Some non-breeding birds may stay and winter in Australia.

Dollarbirds are often seen perched on a branch in a dead tree or on power lines, from where they actively hunt by sallying for insects. They feed on a variety of flying insects taken on the wing, usually above the treetops, in clearings or above water and often hunt in the afternoon until after sunset.

RANGE AND HABITAT: Found in open eucalyptus woodlands and often in outer suburban gardens and parks, also in pasture with scattered remnant trees. Widespread on the east coast, notably in Victoria and New South Wales, in inland Queensland to about Mt. Isa, and in northern Australia. A rare visitor to South Australia and some offshore islands.

BREEDING: Breeds from October to January in tree hollows or termite nests, often near the edges of wetlands. After fledging the young are dependent on their parents for several weeks.

TRACK NO. 30: Raspy cackle or chatter *kek-kek-kek-ek-kek-kek*, single *kek* calls or *yap*, and rapid *yapapapap* calls.

31 | Satin Bowerbird
Ptilonorhynchus violaceus

The adult male Satin Bowerbird is a medium-sized bird with a glossy blue-black plumage, a striking violet-blue iris and a yellow bill, and it is undoubtedly the best-known member of the bowerbird family. Although the adult male is easily identified by its glossy blue-black plumage, this is not attained until its seventh year. Prior to that the birds of each sex resemble each other, having greenish plumage.

Male Satin Bowerbirds are promiscuous, mating with several females during the season. They construct a display bower out of sticks on the forest floor and decorate it with blue and yellow ornaments. The bower is the focal point of a male's display and there he advertises his presence with loud whistles and performs a ritualised sexual dancing display to attract the female into his bower where copulation takes place.

Satin Bowerbirds are omnivorous. Their main diet is fruit, particularly figs, but they also take spiders and insects including beetles, cicadas, moths and caterpillars. They will occasionally take young birds, eggs and lizards to supplement their diet.

RANGE AND HABITAT: Found in a range of habitats from rainforests to suburban gardens, but prefers rainforest edges with a dense understorey. The species' range is restricted to the south-east and eastern Australia and the Wet Tropics region of north-eastern Australia.

BREEDING: The breeding season is from about May to December. Each female mates only once, nests in a tree nearby and incubates the eggs alone.

TRACK NO. 31: A vast array of vocalisations, including buzzing, whirring, rattling, churring, whistling and mimicry of a wide variety of species, including the sounds of a cat, dingo and also some mechanical sounds. Geographical variation in song has also been reported for this species.

32 | Great Bowerbird
Ptilonorhynchus nuchalis

This species is the largest of the bowerbirds and unlike other members of its family is not a forest-dweller *per se* but often inhabits open rocky country with scattered trees and bushes. The Great Bowerbird is widely distributed in northern Australia.

It is mostly uniform pale brown in plumage and has a bright violet-pink crest on the nape, which is used by the male during display. Males build a large two-walled avenue bower for courtship displays and collect many decorations to place at each end of the avenue. These decorations include snail shells, bones, green leaves and fruits, but glass and metal objects are sometimes collected too. The mating success of males seems to correlate with the quality and/or number of particular colour decorations at their bower. Their food mainly consists of fruits and berries of native plants, but is often supplemented with exotic fruits, nectar, seeds, flowers and insects. Young birds are fed a diet of animal matter, consisting of grasshoppers, crickets, caterpillars, beetles and spiders, supplemented with fruits. Sometimes lizards and moths are taken as well.

RANGE AND HABITAT: Found in an extensive range across northern Australia, including some offshore islands. Occurs from the Kimberleys in north-west Western Australia to north Queensland in the east, and from Cape York Peninsula south to Mackay. Inhabits rainforest fringes, vine thickets, open savanna, mangrove fringes and urban gardens.

BREEDING: The males are polygynous and mate with several females during courtship, while the females perform all the nest duties. The breeding season varies throughout the year depending on rainfall, but the main breeding peak seems to be in October and November.

TRACK NO. 32: Highly vocal, giving a variety of harsh calls and mimicry. Also cackles, hisses, whistles and churs. Both sexes are adept at mimicry.

33 | Superb Fairy-wren
Malurus cyaneus

Fairy-wrens among the most popular birds in Australia. Male Superb Fairy-wrens in nuptial plumage are iridescent azure blue on the head, lower back and uppertail-coverts, while females are greyish brown with a pale rufous chin and belly and orange-brown bill. Only the older adult males retain their bright colours throughout the year.

One of the most striking characteristics of this delightful species is its social behaviour. Birds live in cooperative family groups in a permanent territory. These little birds have adapted well to garden life, feeding primarily on small invertebrates, but their numbers are declining in city gardens. Unfortunately they are often preyed upon by domestic cats, while habitat is disappearing due to people having manicured gardens that offer little or no protection to these birds.

Superb Fairy-wrens are notoriously aggressive and territorial when nesting. The males are often seen attacking their reflections in a window, mirror or hubcap of a parked car. They are also very promiscuous, with the females often engaging in illicit extra-pair copulation out of the territory while still engaged to the original partner.

RANGE AND HABITAT: Common in eastern and south-eastern Australia including Tasmania. Found in a range of habitats including woodland, mangroves, shrubland, grassland, parks and gardens.

BREEDING: Nest is a domed structure of grass and rootlets placed low down in dense vegetation. Breeds from June to February and lays 3–4 eggs; incubation period is about 14 days. The young fledge in 10–14 days and often remain with the group as helpers for several years.

TRACK NO. 33: A musical trill and reel of song delivered throughout the day, more often during the breeding season. Alarm call is a sharp *chit* or 'churring.' Females also sing to defend their territory against other females.

34 | Variegated Fairy-wren
Malurus lamberti

A shy and often elusive bird of low shrubbery. Long tail usually held erect. Male slightly larger and much more colourful than the brownish female.

Resident pairs or groups defend territory. Most helpers are the progeny from earlier years that remain in the family group after they reach sexual maturity. They are predominantly insectivorous.

RANGE AND HABITAT: Inhabits dense shrubby vegetation, from coastal heathland to thickets in broken rocky country, and creek-side shrubbery to the semi-arid and arid interior of Australia.

BREEDING: Breeds from July to December. Domed nest of grass and flaky bark is bound by cobwebs and lined with fur, feathers or fine plant material. The female alone builds the nest and lays three eggs, but all group members help to feed the nestlings.

TRACK NO. 34: Songs, or 'reels,' include regular repetition of phrases. All group members indulge in song. Contact call is a short, very high-pitched *tee*. Alarm call is a harsh, rallying, chattering *zzzat, zzzat zzzat*. Sings most often in early morning and late afternoon.

35 | White-browed Scrubwren
Sericornis frontalis

A familiar small brown bird with a blackish mask, white throat and with a white stripe over the yellow eye. Ten different subspecies are recognised in Australia. They are inquisitive and confiding,

A sedentary, cooperative breeder, usually found singly or in pairs, sometimes in small parties. Usually forages among leaf-litter under low shrubs. Diet includes worms, other invertebrates, seeds and berries.

RANGE AND HABITAT: Abundant from northern Queensland along the east and south coasts to Western Australia. Favours thick undergrowth, often found near human habitation.

BREEDING: Breeds throughout the year but mostly from August to January. Nest is a well-hidden dome of grass and leaves on the ground with a side entrance, often placed near the vertical side of a tree, bank or gully.

TRACK NO. 35: Call notes include a sharp whistle, a loud *wizzit-wizzit-wizzit*, trilling and buzzing alarm calls and also a kind of pumping call sounding like *tsi-tsi-tsi* or *tseer-tseer-tseer*. Also an accomplished mimic.

36 | Yellow-rumped Thornbill
Acanthiza chrysorrhoa

Easily recognisable thanks to its black crown with fine white spotting, white eyebrow, pale eye and bright yellow rump which is conspicuous in flight. Most thornbills are sociable birds, and in the non-breeding season they are often found in small flocks and in the company of other insect-eating birds. Yellow-rumped is terrestrial in its foraging habits and feeds primarily on small insects, worms, arthropods and seeds.

RANGE AND HABITAT: Wide distribution across the southern half of Australia including Tasmania. Prefers all kinds of open country, short grassland with shrubs, farmland, urban parks and golf courses.

BREEDING: Builds a remarkable two-storey nest consisting of a domed main chamber with a side entrance and a cup-shaped structure on top. Breeds from July to December. This is another cooperative breeding species in which the young from previous years help to feed the brood. Nest often parasitised by Shining Bronze-Cuckoo.

TRACK NO. 36: The song is a pleasant, bell-like, tinkling sound. The flight calls are an abrupt *zip-zip-zip* call.

37 | Brown Thornbill
Acanthiza pusilla

This species is often found, singly or in pairs, among the foliage of eucalypts or in low undergrowth near creeks, feeding on a variety of insects and arthropods. Readily recognised by buff scalloped forehead and brown to reddish-brown rump, which contrasts with the olive-brown upperparts. The breast and throat are heavily streaked and white-tipped tail has a dark sub-terminal band. Red eye distinguishes this species from most of the other thornbills in its range except Tasmanian.

RANGE AND HABITAT: Occurs from south-east Queensland down the east coast and across to Adelaide, as well as Tasmania.

BREEDING: Breeds from July to December. Nest is a domed oval structure with a side entrance, built of grass, leaves and spiders' webs in a prickly bush or bracken close to the ground.

TRACK NO. 37: The song is a pleasant warble and chatter and often includes mimicry. When alarmed utters buzzing and scolding calls.

38 | Spotted Pardalote
Pardalotus punctatus

Pardalotes are family of small landbirds which is endemic to Australia. The Spotted Pardalote, sometimes also called a 'bank diamond' or 'diamond bird,' is one of the most colourful members of this genus. It is the smallest species of the group, but also arguably the most attractive with its black crown, wings and tail all heavily spotted with white. The face is grey with a white stripe above the eye. The throat and underparts are golden yellow, the rump is crimson and the abdomen light fawn. The female is similarly marked but lacks the yellow throat of the male and the spots on her head are pale yellow instead of white.

Usually seen in pairs, but sometimes small parties forage for food in the outer foliage of tall trees. Diet consists of scale insects, thrips, lerps, spiders, moths and many other small invertebrates, but also includes manna and honeydew.

RANGE AND HABITAT: Range includes most of eastern Australia down to Tasmania and across the south to south-west Western Australia. Usually found in open or heavily timbered country. It is a particularly common garden bird in eastern Australia, where it can be found frequenting eucalyptus trees.

BREEDING: The breeding season is from August to December and the eggs are laid in a nesting chamber in a hollow branch or tree trunk. It also nests in tunnels about a metre deep, which are dug into earth banks and often beside watercourses or on the ground.

TRACK NO. 38: The two- to three-note song of the Spotted Pardalote can be described as *tu-teetee-tit* and is highly ventriloquial; its contact calls are a soft *dee-dee*.

39 | Striated Pardalote
Pardalotus striatus

This species has a number of distinct forms and together the distributions of these cover almost the entire continent of Australia. All have mainly black wings and tail, grey back and a yellowish throat. The underparts are predominantly white at the centre, blending into fawn on the flanks. In some forms a yellow stripe above the eye merges into white at the nape. A red spot on the wing can be seen at close range.

More northerly forms tend to have a plain black crown and eye-stripe, while the southerly forms tend to have white striations on the crown and ear-covert. There is, however, considerable overlap in the distributions of these forms and some of the stripe-crowned birds have been found to interbreed with the black-crowned birds where their ranges overlap.

Northern and western forms of Striated Pardalote have a wide bar of six to seven white-edged primary feathers on the wing, while the southern and eastern forms have a narrow bar of three or four whitish primaries.

RANGE AND HABITAT: Common and widespread in suitable eucalyptus forest and woodland habitat covering the entire continent of Australia, including Tasmania and coastal islands.

Breeding: Nesting habits are fairly consistent throughout this group and all of them either excavate small tunnels in sandbanks or road cuttings or use hollows in trees or tree stumps. The tunnels are dug to a depth of 50–60cm by both sexes, first by opening the ground with their bill and then, as the hole gets bigger, excavating by scratching with both feet. They usually breed from June to February and lay a clutch of 2–5 white eggs.

TRACK NO. 39: Common calls include *pick-wick*, *be quick* and *witt-a-witta* and these are often the only way of identifying these birds high in the treetops.

40 | Eastern Spinebill
Acanthorhynchus tenuirostris

The two spinebill species are honeyeaters with a long, slender downcurved bills which are used to effectively forage and probe for nectar from all sorts of flowers.

The male Eastern Spinebill has crown, wings and rump blue-grey. Breast white with a rufous throat-patch and black border. Eye red, nape rufous and belly buff. Female's plumage brownish-buff and less distinctive.

Spinebills are active, fast-moving birds which constantly search for nectar-producing flowers, particularly banksias, grevillias and eucalypts. They feed on nectar, pollen and invertebrates such as spiders and flying insects.

RANGE AND HABITAT: Has an extensive distribution throughout the Great Dividing Range from northern Queensland down to south-east Victoria and Tasmania, and west to south-east South Australia.

BREEDING: Breeds from August to December. Nest constructed from materials such as grass, leaves and cobwebs.

TRACK NO. 40: Call notes include a high-pitched piping *tee-tee-tee*, and rapidly repeated twittering.

41 | Western Spinebill
Acanthorhynchus superciliosus

Superficially similar in structure and appearance to the Eastern Spinebill, but the ranges of the two species do not overlap. Both sexes of the Western Spinebill have plain creamy underparts and plain brown-grey upperparts except for a rufous nape and white supercilium behind the eye. The male has a rufous throat patch, which is larger than that of its close relative, and a black mask and a black band across the breast.

RANGE AND HABITAT: The Western Spinebill has a limited distribution in woodland, scrub and heathland in the south-west corner of Western Australia.

BREEDING: Breeds from September to January. Builds a cup-nest mainly out of grass, which is situated low in a bush or tree.

TRACK NO. 41: Most commonly heard calls are a high-pitched *kweet-kweet*.

42 | Lewin's Honeyeater
Meliphaga lewinii

Mostly olive-green with a decurved blackish bill and bluish iris. Prominent yellow-white gape extends below eye and has a bold yellow crescent ear-tuft. Fearless, inquisitive and extremely aggressive towards other honeyeaters. Usually seen singly or in pairs, sometimes in small flocks where food is abundant. Favoured foods are berries and fruit, also takes nectar and insects.

RANGE AND HABITAT: Occurs in wet forests, riparian vegetation and coastal scrub in eastern Australia from Cooktown in north Queensland east of the Great Dividing Range down to Melbourne in Victoria. Seldom seen far from dense cover. Often raids orchards and seen in parks and gardens looking for food scraps.

BREEDING: Breeds from August to January. Nest is a large, flimsy cup made of bark strips, leaves, grass and moss bound together with spiders' webs.

TRACK NO. 42: Best field characteristic is distinct, far-carrying, rolling staccato call, sometimes likened to machine-gun fire. Also a single note *toc* or *chot* repeated rather slowly at regular intervals, a repeated loud and harsh scolding *schwep*, and a harsh *tchuuu*.

43 | Singing Honeyeater
Lichenostomus versicolor

Medium-sized, olive-brown above with pale underparts. Has a conspicuous black band through the eye and running down the side of neck, with a yellow streak below ending in a yellow-white tuft.

Its name is a misnomer as it rarely sings and the song is not very musical. Loud duet-singing by pairs from prominent perches may account for the name.

Intolerant towards other honeyeaters. Usually forages close to ground on a wide range of insects, fruits and nectar, sometimes augments its diet with Zebra Finch eggs.

RANGE AND HABITAT: Widespread throughout mainland Australia. The most common honeyeater inland. Generally absent east of the Great Dividing Range and in the far north. Occurs in a range of open habitats ranging from arid scrubland to open woodlands. A common garden bird in Perth.

BREEDING: Breeds from July to February. Untidy nest of grass, rootlets and other plant material usually placed in a thick bush.

TRACK NO. 43: Varied, with clear and loud calls described as *sheek, terik-terik*; also resonant trilling notes.

44 | Yellow-faced Honeyeater
Lichenostomus chrysops

The only honeyeater with obvious migratory patterns. Each year from March to May thousands move north into Queensland from the south, with flocks of up to 100 birds following defined flight-paths. Weather patterns can lead to so-called 'nonsense migration,' with the birds moving first north, then south again, sometimes west. Some resident and sedentary populations remain in the south during winter.

Plumage generally olive-brown with an obvious yellow facial stripe extending below and behind the eye. Feeds on insects, nectar, manna, pollen, seeds, berries and fruit.

RANGE AND HABITAT: Widespread in eastern Australia from northern Queensland to south-east South Australia. Occurs in a wide variety of habitats including woodlands and heathlands and is a frequent visitor to urban parks and gardens.

BREEDING: Breeding season mostly from October to January. Builds a cup-shaped nest made of fine bark strips.

TRACK NO. 44: Contact calls *chick-up, chick-up, chick-up* and song similar or a more stereotyped *chee-chitty, di-chitty tee tee*, also short plaintive *peep* and *kheer* calls.

45 | White-plumed Honeyeater
Lichenostomus penicillatus

Mainly olive-green, richly tinged with yellow – known colloquially as the 'greenie.' Bold white neck-plume is diagnostic.

A vigorous and noisy bird, dashing about in swift erratic flights through the foliage. Sedentary and lives in colonies, with the birds sometimes becoming aggressive and defending their food sources from other bird species. Diet consists mainly of insects, pollen and nectar.

RANGE AND HABITAT: Common and widespread endemic found in coastal scrub, open forest, and particularly near watercourses. Absent from some eastern coastal regions, Tasmania, tropical northern Australia and southern parts of Western Australia and South Australia. The most common honeyeater in inner urban areas of Sydney, Melbourne and Adelaide.

BREEDING: Breeds mainly from July to January. The nest is a deep cup of bark fibres, grasses and cobwebs, suspended at the end of the finest twigs of a eucalyptus tree

TRACK NO. 45: Display flight calls are *chick-o-wee*, alarm and warning calls are a high-pitched and rapid trill *tchee-tcheee-tchee*.

46 | Noisy Miner
Manorina melanocephala

The Noisy Miner is a native Australian honeyeater which is grey and brown in colour with a white forehead, black crown and cheeks, a yellow bill, a patch of yellow behind the eyes and yellow legs. Its name is often confused with that of the Common Myna, *Acridotheres tristis*, which is an introduced species of Asian starling.

The Noisy Miner is known colloquially as the 'soldier bird' or 'mickey bird.' It is sedentary and lives in sometimes very large colonies, where it is often conspicuous due to its noisy and pugnacious behaviour. Most honeyeaters are aggressive but the Noisy Miner is notorious for its unrelenting group aggression, directed towards all bird species and many animals. Groups of Noisy Miners exclude nearly all other birds from the area. Noisy Miners are cooperative breeders and actively collaborate in territorial defence, hunting and feeding and unite to ward off any intruder. It is primarily an insectivorous honeyeater, but will also feed on nectar and honeydew.

RANGE AND HABITAT: The Noisy Miner is common throughout the eucalyptus forest and woodland of eastern Australia and is typically a species that inhabits fragmented landscape. It has a wide distribution, occurring throughout temperate and sub-tropical eastern Australia, typically where eucalypts occur adjacent to grassy clearings. Common in gardens in cities such as Sydney.

BREEDING: Breeding is from June to December, but in Queensland year-round. The nest is a very flimsy, often transparent cup made of grass and rootlets, bound with cobwebs and lined with hair, fur or wool.

TRACK NO. 46: A wide variety of whistling and chuckling calls. Territorial calls, *tue-teu-teu-teu* uttered in flight. Their piercing alarm calls alert members of the group, and also warn other species.

BACKYARD BIRD SOUNDS | 39

47 | Little Wattlebird
Anthochaera chrysoptera

The name Little Wattlebird is something of a misnomer as this species lacks wattles. Two forms of the species occur in Australia: the Little Wattlebird, *A.c.chrysoptera*, of the east and south coasts; and the Western Wattlebird, *A.c.lunulata*, of the south-west coast. Today the latter is afforded full species status by many authorities.

Little and Western Wattlebirds look very similar. Both are dull brown and heavily streaked, and they have a conspicuous chestnut-orange colour on the primaries, which shows in flight but is concealed when the bird is at rest. Sexes are similar in appearance but the male is slightly larger. Western lacks heavy streaking on the crown and back, and the voices also differ substantially.

Feeds primarily on pollen, manna and nectar but will also take small invertebrates and fruits. Outside the breeding season it tends to be sociable and occurs in flocks, particularly where banksias are in flower.

RANGE AND HABITAT: Little Wattlebird occurs from south-east Queensland to South Australia and Tasmania. Western Wattlebird is found in south-west Western Australia, where it is usually confined to the coast. Inhabits heathland, shrubland dominated by banksias, dry sclerophyll forest, coastal fore dunes with dense shrubbery and urban environments with parks and gardens.

BREEDING: Breeds from June to December, nest cup-shaped and built in a fork of a bush or tree at varying heights. It is a loose structure of long fine twigs and is lined with fine material.

TRACK NO. 47: Track begins with Little Wattlebirds from eastern Australia. Includes rapid trisyllabic, harsh call sounding like *biddy-quock* or *cookaycock*. Dawn song is a rapid *tee-tee-tee-au-err* interspersed with *backoff-backoff-backoff*. Calls during the day vary and song also as *kock-kock-keck-keck* repeated rapidly or *kecko-kecko-kecko-keck* repeated rapidly four times. Track ends with chattering sounds of Western Wattlebird.

48 | Red Wattlebird
Anthocaera carunculata

A large brownish streaked honeyeater with two brilliant red wattles hanging like earrings just behind the eyes. Has a long white-tipped tail and a yellow abdomen. Aggressive during the breeding season, but otherwise sociable and forms large, raucous flocks that feed high in flowering trees. Feeds on fruit, insects, pollen and nectar.

RANGE AND HABITAT: Common and widespread from south-east Queensland down the east coast to Victoria and along the southern coast to south-west Western Australia. Occurs in a wide range of habitats from alpine forest, lowland forests, open woodland, coastal heathland with banksias and urban areas. A common bird in many parks and gardens, even in cities such as Perth and Sydney.

BREEDING: Breeds mostly from July and August. Nest is a large untidy open cup of bark, sticks and leaves.

TRACK NO. 48: During breeding season calls *tjucke-tjucke-tjuck* at daybreak. Also utters single guttural croaks and other loud harsh calls, cackles, whistling calls, and bill-snapping.

49 | Brown Honeyeater
Lichmera indistincta

Plumage greyish-brown above, with olive-green on the wings, grey underparts and a tiny patch of yellow-white feathers behind the eye. Bill comparatively long and decurved to access the nectar in tubular flowers. Most Brown Honeyeaters have a yellow gape, and only adult males in the breeding season develop a black gape. Feeds primarily on nectar and a variety of insects.

RANGE AND HABITAT: Most of Australia, but excluding Victoria, South Australia and Tasmania. Considered resident but some southern populations are migratory. Inhabits heathland, savanna woodland, riverine forest, mallee, mangroves, rainforest edges, arid and semi-arid zones and urban areas, where it visits parks and gardens.

BREEDING: Breeds from June to January. Builds a small cup-shaped nest from bark and grasses, suspended from the branches of a shrub or tree. Nest often parasitised by the Pallid Cuckoo.

TRACK NO. 49: Song is reminiscent of that of the Australian Reed-Warbler, being metallic and musical. Warning and signal calls are harsh, contact calls are a series of *plick* notes.

50 | New Holland Honeyeater
Phylidonyris novaehollandiae

A boldly marked honeyeater associated with heathland, flowering banksias and other native shrubs. It is mainly black and white with heavily streaked underparts and shows a conspicuous white eye. The head is black with three white patches and a white 'eyebrow' high on the crown. The blackish tail has yellow at the base and the large yellow patches on the wings were reflected in its old name of 'Yellow-winged Honeyeater,' although several other honeyeater species have similar yellow wing-patches. The common name New Holland Honeyeater is simply derived from the bird's scientific name, but a more appropriate name would perhaps have been 'White-bearded Honeyeater,' since the white stripes on the throat give it a bearded effect. The long brushy tongue is efficiently used to gather pollen and nectar from nectar-bearing trees. Also feeds on a variety of insects, lerps, nectar, manna, honeydew, fruit and berries.

RANGE AND HABITAT: Widespread and common in eastern, southern and south-western coastal areas of Australia, including Tasmania and coastal islands in the Bass Strait. Found in a variety of habitats, including heathland, timbered country with dense shrubs, and gardens, particularly where there are flowering native shrubs.

BREEDING: Breeds throughout the year, with timing being heavily influenced by the abundance of flowering plants. Nesting usually occurs when banksias come into flower. Nest is a cup made from bark-fibres, twigs and cobwebs and lined with grasses, animal hair, feathers or other soft material, and placed in a low shrub or small tree. Both sexes share in nest construction, incubation and feeding of young.

TRACK NO. 50: A metallic high-frequency song, whistles, loud *chick-chick* calls and a loud chattering alarm call. Also has a complex flight-song uttered by the male.

51 | Noisy Friarbird
Phelemon corniculatus

This bird, sometimes called 'leatherhead,' is one of the comics of the Australian bush. Not only does it have a bizarre appearance, but its voice is also a strange jumble of notes. A large aggressive honeyeater. Plumage grey-brown with a prominent knob on top of the bill, and a bare head with black skin. Sexes similar. Social and pugnacious towards other birds. Feeds on insects, eggs, pollen, nectar, berries and native and cultivated fruit; can become very destructive in orchards.

RANGE AND HABITAT: Common in eastern coastal regions from Cape York Peninsula in Queensland to the inland of southern Victoria. Southern birds migrate north during winter. Occurs in urban areas, orchards, parks, gardens, sclerophyll forest, open woodland and along watercourses.

BREEDING: Breeds from August to January. Nest is an open cup of bark or grass suspended from a drooping branch, commonly over water.

TRACK NO. 51: A wide variety of calls and song. Very raucous when in large numbers, in feeding flocks a continual babble, which sounds like *four-o-clock* or *chock-chock*.

52 | Blue-faced Honeyeater
Entomyzon cyanotis

Named after the large patch of bare blue skin around the eye (green in immatures). Beautiful plumage boldy marked black, white and golden-olive. Often called 'banana bird' in Queensland, they have become a pest in certain fruit-growing areas where they raid orchards. Actively feed on a wide variety of fruits and berries, insects, lizards, pollen and nectar and are usually seen feeding amongst flowering native trees, extracting nectar with their long brushy-tipped tongues.

RANGE AND HABITAT: Found from north-east Western Australia, across the north and down the east coast into Victoria. Forages in well-timbered country, open woodland, farmland, *Pandanus*, paperbark forest, gardens, golf courses and orchards, rarely far from water.

BREEDING: Breeds from June to January. Nest is a deep cup made from bark strips and rootlets, lined with soft material. Also uses old nests of other birds.

TRACK NO. 52: This species has a poor voice and call with a loud ascending *kwip* or *hu-ieett* whistle, repeated several times, also scolding calls.

53 | Black-faced Cuckoo-shrike
Coracina novaehollandiae

A familiar and distinctive pale grey bird with a long blue-grey tail. Adults have a black face and throat while immatures have a black patch from bill to ear-coverts. The flight is undulating and on landing they have a habit of shuffling their wings. Feeds mainly on a variety of insects.

RANGE AND HABITAT: Widespread throughout Australia, including Tasmania. A partial migrant; some populations sedentary, others migrating north to New Guinea, the Solomon Islands or Indonesia after breeding. Occupies a wide variety of forested habitats, including open woodland, dry sclerophyll forest, farmland, low shrubland, open pasture, urban areas, towns, parks and gardens.

BREEDING: Breeds from August to February. Nest is a small saucer-shaped platform of twigs and spiders' webs placed on a horizontal fork of a branch. Both sexes share the nest-building.

TRACK NO. 53: A metallic, rolling, churring note and croaky *prurr*, but also a higher-pitched *chereer-chereer-chereer-chereer* call in flight.

54 | White-bellied Cuckoo-shrike
Coracina papuensis

At first sight resembles a small immature Black-faced Cuckoo-shrike. However, the area of black on the face does not extend behind the eye. Usually occurs singly or in pairs, but found in small flocks outside the breeding season. Usually perches unobtrusively in trees and is only detected by diagnostic call. Appears to be more common in north Australia.

Feeds primarily on a variety of insects gleaned from foliage or taken in the air. Diet also includes caterpillars, fruit and nectar.

RANGE AND HABITAT: Generally sedentary. Occurs from the Kimberleys east along the northern coastal belt and through eastern dry regions south to Victoria and south-eastern South Australia. Widespread and frequents many types of woodland and forest as well as urban areas and suburban gardens.

BREEDING: Breeds from August to March. Nest is a shallow cup of bark and twigs.

TRACK NO. 54: Main call is a diagnostic squeaky *kisseek*, often uttered in flight, another is a *churr* or churring call.

55 | Grey Shrike-thrush
Colluricincla harmonica

One of the best and most melodious songsters in Australia. Inquisitive and often fearless of humans. Plumage fairly plain grey and buff; bill robust with a tiny hook at the tip. Feeds mainly on small invertebrates but will also take nestlings, eggs, small mammals, lizards, frogs, snails, fruit and seeds.

RANGE AND HABITAT: Resident. Habitat variable; found in open woodland, scrubland, golf courses, parks and gardens, and on the outskirts of rainforest edges. Common throughout Australia, except in central desert.

BREEDING: Breeds from July to February, and in arid regions after heavy rain. Cup-shaped nest placed in a fork, dense vegetation, crevice or hollow tree. Sexes share in nest-building, incubation, care of young and defence of territory.

TRACK NO. 55: A number of loud melodious whistling calls, which show considerable geographical variation. Both male and female sing throughout the year, and often duet. Alarm call is a harsh wheezing and in the winter they give a ringing or *yorrick* call. Also mimics.

56 | Green Figbird
Sphecotheres vieilloti

Male olive-green with grey or yellow underparts (depending on race), black head and bare red skin around the eye, which can become brilliantly red in an instant when aggressive. Female dull brown and heavily streaked with bare grey-brown skin around the eye.

Found in pairs during breeding season, but generally lives in small flocks close to fruiting trees. Also feeds on insects, seeds and nectar.

RANGE AND HABITAT: Occurs in coastal northern and eastern Australia southwards to Bega in New South Wales. Found in urban areas and a wide range of other habitats, including rainforest, eucalypt forest, riparian forest, woodland, paperbark forest and mangroves.

BREEDING: Breeds from October to February. Nest is an open cup made of fine twigs, vine tendrils and grass on a horizontal fork near the end of a branch. The female alone builds the nest.

TRACK NO. 56: A variety of whistles, loud, clear, slightly descending *see-kew, see-kew*, also down-slurred whistle *tchieuw*, chirping notes and raucous chattering from flocks.

57 | Yellow Oriole
Oriolus flavocinctus

58 | Olive-backed Oriole
Oriolus sagittatus

Two species of oriole occur in Australia. Both have red eyes and a red bill. The Yellow Oriole is yellowish-green all over, including on the underparts. The upperparts of both sexes are variably streaked black and the dark wing-feathers have bold yellow borders. The male is fairly plain green and yellow on the head and underparts while the female has dark streaking. Feeds on fruit and invertebrates.

RANGE AND HABITAT: Occurs in coastal areas of northern parts of Western Australia, Northern Territory and Queensland. Nomadic and follows the fruiting of various trees, utilising a variety of habitats including rainforest, woodland, paperbark and mangroves.

BREEDING: Breeds from September to January. Builds a cup-shaped nest from fibres, grass and leaves bound with spiders' webs, which is suspended in a fork in a tree from a horizontal branch.

TRACK NO. 57: Sings *tolong-tolong*, also a harsh mewing call. Can mimic other species.

Similar in size and structure to Yellow Oriole, and like that species has olive head and mantle and red bill and eyes. However, the underparts of the Olive-backed Oriole lack any olive or yellow tones and instead are white with blackish streaks. Diet similar to Yellow Oriole. Most often seen singly or in pairs.

RANGE AND HABITAT: Occurs across northern Australia, down the east coast from Cape York to Victoria and as far west as Adelaide. Migratory in southern parts of range and found as far west as the Great Dividing Range. Like the Yellow Oriole it is nomadic in the north of the range as it searches for fruiting trees and can be found in a number of different woodland and forest habitats.

BREEDING: Breeds from September to January. Cup-shaped nest suspended in a tree and built using grass and other plant materials.

TRACK NO. 58: Typical song is *ori-ole* or *eee-ole*. Also an accomplished mimic.

59 | Black Butcherbird
Cracticus quoyi

Australia's largest butcherbird, glossy black in colour (young birds brown) with a massive pale blue-grey bill which is hooked at the tip; hard to confuse with any other bird. Sexes similar. Sedentary, highly territorial and aggressive, particularly during breeding season. Secretive, more often heard than seen in dense foliage.

Forages on ground in vegetation for invertebrates, small animals, birds and their eggs, and fruits. Sometimes forages in suburban areas and on ground in garden flower-beds.

RANGE AND HABITAT: In Australia occurs from north-east coast of Western Australia, across coastal areas of Northern Territory, to Ingham and Mackay in Queensland. Found in dense rainforest, mangroves, monsoon forests with vine thickets and woodlands.

BREEDING: Breeds before wet season from September to January. Nest is a cup of twigs in a forked branch high in a tree.

TRACK NO. 59: Loud, far-carrying and rich *aah-ooh*. Has other melodious songs and calls, although these vary geographically. Often calls before dawn.

60 | Grey Butcherbird
Cracticus torquatus

A small but well-known butcherbird. Mantle grey, head, wings and tail black, whitish below, with a strong hooked bill. It is a predator of small birds, which usually avoid the immediate vicinity of the butcherbird's territory. Also feeds on insects, rodents, reptiles and fruit. Often perches quietly on a branch watching for prey on the ground.

RANGE AND HABITAT: It is widespread throughout Australia but absent from Cape York Peninsula and arid desert regions. Inhabits open eucalypt forests and woodlands with dense to patchy understorey, urban areas and townships. Often common in gardens.

BREEDING: Breeds from July to January. Nest is an untidy, shallow, open bowl-shaped structure, with a well-formed cup mostly made of fine dead twigs, lined with rootlets and other soft materials.

TRACK NO. 60: A splendid songster which often sings in a duet. Has a variety of calls including caroling, musical whistles and mimicry, but considerable geographical variation. Most often calls during spring, less in other seasons.

61 | Pied Butcherbird
Cracticus nigrogularis

The Pied Butcherbird is a conspicuous and familiar bird in many areas. In appearance it looks like a small magpie, with sharp contrasting black and white plumage, a black hood and chest, and a blue-grey bill that is strongly hooked at the tip.

Lives in small family groups and is highly territorial, occupying the same territory for many years.

Butcherbirds are an efficient predator of small birds and one of the habits practised by them is to impale prey which too big to swallow on a fork in a tree or on a sharp twig or thorn; hence the name butcherbird. They are usually seen singly or in pairs, sometimes in small groups, and feed on a variety of insects, rodents, reptiles, nestlings, small birds and sometimes fruit.

RANGE AND HABITAT: Distributed throughout mainland Australia except for the arid deserts, heavy forested areas and the south-west and south-east coasts. It is a resident in a wide variety of habitats, including open woodland, scrubland, farmland and pastoral country. Much of its habitat overlaps with the Grey Butcherbird, but the Pied prefers the more open country and its distribution tends to be more northerly.

BREEDING: Breeds from July to December. The nest is a deep open cup mostly made of twigs and sticks and lined with rootlets, animal hair, wool, fur, grass or feathers.

TRACK NO. 61: This is one of Australia's best songsters, often duetting, with a varied repertoire of loud whistles. It is also sometimes called the 'organ bird' and the synchronisation in its duets is so precise that one cannot tell when one bird stops and the other begins. They are also exquisite mimics and ventriloquists.

62 | Australian Magpie
Cracticus tibicen

The Australian Magpie is one of the best-known birds in Australia because of its ferocious attacks on people who stray anywhere near its nest during the breeding season. This can make these birds rather unpopular in places such as golf courses, parks and school playgrounds.

Magpies are large black and white birds which are sociable and live in groups. They are strongly territorial all the year round and will defend their territory cooperatively. They have adapted well to human settlement and are common in agricultural and suburban areas. Magpies occur throughout Australia with three distinct forms: The black-backed, white-backed and western forms. These forms all interbreed where their ranges overlap and their offspring are fertile. As a consequence they are regarded as a single species.

Magpies are omnivorous and feed on frogs, lizards, small birds, invertebrates, carrion, rodents, grain and even garbage. Many city-dwelling magpies exploit the generous food trays provided by humans.

RANGE AND HABITAT: Widespread throughout Australia and Tasmania, except at the tip of Cape York Peninsula, the northern parts of the Northern Territory and in the arid deserts. Mainly occurs in open habitat, open woodland and common in towns, cities, parks and gardens with lawns.

BREEDING: Breeding season variable but extends from June to November. Although the males are sexually mature in their first year, they have to wait several years to attain breeding status in the group and acquire a territory. The nest, a bulky structure, is usually placed high in a eucalypt tree and is a basket of sticks and twigs lined with grass, hair, or other soft material.

TRACK NO. 62: The song is beautiful and distinctive. A melodious fluting carol, sometimes heard on a moonlit night, soft descending whistles and organ-like caroling, warbling song. Also adept at mimicry.

63 | Spangled Drongo
Dicrurus bracteatus

Glossy black with a greenish sheen, heavy bill, red eye and forked tail (an important identification feature). Omnivorous, feeding primarily on insects, but will also feed on nectar, pollen and fruit, sometimes also young birds or bats. Can be destructive near beehives.

RANGE AND HABITAT: Widespread from north Western Australia to northern Queensland and southwards to eastern Victoria. Some populations are migratory and winter in Papua New Guinea and the Solomon Islands, while others move southwards to winter into Victoria and central New South Wales. Occurs in a wide variety of habitats, including rainforest, monsoon forest, vine thickets, sclerophyll forests, riverine woodland, mangroves, open country and parks and gardens.

BREEDING: Breeds from September to March. Nest is an open cup in a fork of a slender horizontal branch of a bushy tree.

TRACK NO. 63: An accomplished mimic which perfectly imitates many different species. Harsh twanging sounds *dududueeing*, a variety of whistles, chattering and squeaks. Very noisy and often calls while perched or in flight.

64 | Pied Currawong
Strepera graculina

A large black bird with a robust black bill and yellow eyes. The white rump and white wing-patches are conspicuous in flight. The undertail-coverts and tail-tip are also white. An altitudinal migrant in the south, breeding in mountain forests and migrating to lowlands in winter, forming large flocks and often visiting cities in search of food. Feeds on fruit, seeds, small birds, eggs, invertebrates, rodents, reptiles and garbage.

RANGE AND HABITAT: Restricted to the eastern parts of the continent from Cape York in Queensland south to south-western Victoria and south-eastern South Australia. Occurs in alpine forests, woodland, open plains, coastal scrub, farmland, cities and towns.

BREEDING: Breeds in solitary pairs along the Great Dividing Range from August to December. Builds a bulky nest from sticks and twigs.

TRACK NO. 64: A wide variety of calls and geographical variation in song also apparent. Loud descending *currawong*, also *crik*, *crik*, a wolf-whistle *weeeeooo*, whistles, sometimes a mewing note. Also engages in communal song, a mournful far-carrying chorus.

65 | Grey Fantail
Rhipidura albiscapa

A small grey bird with a white throat, brownish wings with white barring, a grey-black band across the breast and a white eyebrow. The underparts are buff to white and the tail is fan-shaped with white edgings. The Grey Fantail has recently been 'split' from the New Zealand Fantail, *R fuliginosa*, as a separate species and the two have very different vocalisations. Unlike the Willie Wagtail the Grey Fantail is a forest dweller, but during the winter months it can often be found in parks and gardens. Although small, they are conspicuous and vocal throughout the year. The Grey Fantail is well adapted for capturing tiny insects on the wing. They are an extremely active, inquisitive and friendly garden visitor, spending a good deal of their time zigzagging in the air in pursuit of insects. Its flight is erratic as it hawks in the forest or shrub canopy searching for insects. Like most fantails is never still for long and characteristically wags its whole body from side to side, continually flicking its wings and fanning its tail.

RANGE AND HABITAT: Widely distributed in timbered country throughout Australia, including Tasmania. As well as forests, also found in orchards, farms, parks and gardens.

BREEDING: Breeding season is from July to January. Both sexes build the cup-shaped nest, which is usually sited on a thin branch, and from the bottom of which hangs a long thin tail. It is constructed of plant fibres held together with spiders' webs. The nests are often parasitised by some of the small cuckoos.

TRACK NO. 65: Song has a twittering quality and is an extremely high-pitched squeaky ascending series of notes. Sweet musical trilling and chattering.

66 | Willie Wagtail
Rhipidura leucophrys

This resident black and white bird is one of the most common and familiar species in Australian parks and gardens. It is a species of fantail which feeds almost entirely on insects. Often quite fearless and common in towns, suburban gardens and on farms where they are often found associated with grazing stock. Their favourite habitats appear to be fairly open areas such as partly cleared farmland, lightly timbered park-like country and lightly timbered watercourses. It is a restless bird which constantly fans its tail and wags it from side to side. Willie Wagtails are strongly territorial and will drive off any intruder. They are often seen harassing, without fear, much bigger birds, such as kookaburras, hawks and eagles. Diet mainly consist of small insects which are caught on the wing or in trees.

RANGE AND HABITAT: Distribution covers most of Australia. Absent from only a few areas in the deserts of central Australia and dense rainforests. Occurs in most woodland areas, often near watercourses, orchards, suburban parks, gardens and cities.

BREEDING: Three clutches each of three eggs are usual in a breeding season lasting from July to February. The nest is a soft cup-shaped structure built of grass, pieces of bark, hair and other material, woven and bound with spiders' webs. The nest is usually located on a horizontal branch, but nests have been found in woolsheds, on verandahs or in shrubs close to a building.

TRACK NO. 66: Song is interpreted as a rapid *sweet-pretty-little-creature* repeated over and over. During breeding season often sings on moonlit nights. Also makes a harsh chattering alarm call, sounding like *chicka-chicka-chicka*, not unlike the rattle of a half-empty matchbox.

67 | Australian Raven
Corvus coronoides

All five species of Australian crows and ravens look very similar, being large glossy black birds with pale eyes. The most reliable identification feature is their calls and sometimes also their distribution. Feeds on carrion, grubs, insects, grasshoppers, lizards, young birds and eggs.

RANGE AND HABITAT: Distribution covers south-west Western Australia east to Victoria, New South Wales and the southern and western parts of Queensland to the Gulf of Carpentaria. A bird of open country, rarely foraging in forests. Has benefited greatly from development of the pastoral industry and agriculture, which have provided extra food and watering resources. Also adapted well to urban life and good at utilising food sources such as household garbage.

BREEDING: Breeds throughout its range from July to September. Does not breed until three or more years old, pairs for life and remains in the same territory for many years.

TRACK NO. 67: Call is a powerful characteristic *aah-aah-aaaahh*, the last note drawn out and dropping in pitch and intensity. Sometimes also single or double *aah* calls.

68 | Torresian Crow
Corvus orru

Crows are smaller than ravens, have white rather than grey body feathers and lack the ravens' long throat hackles. Their calls are also diagnostic. The Torresian Crow is omnivorous, feeding on a variety of crops, carrion, grubs, insects, grasshoppers, lizards, young birds and eggs. Sometimes seen stealing golf balls which they have mistaken for eggs.

RANGE AND HABITAT: Widespread over much of the tropical northern half of the continent, overlapping their range with the Little Crow and the Australian Raven in Queensland. The Torresian Crow prefers sparse open woodland, areas close to inland creeks and rivers, open pasture and agricultural areas where water is available.

BREEDING: Breeds from August to October. Nests situated on tree, transmission tower, old windmill or cliff ledge. Sedentary, pairs for life and does not breed until at least three years old, remaining in the same territory for many years.

TRACK NO. 68: Typical call notes are a short and abrupt *ackk-ackk-ackk*, but utters a wide variety of calls.

69 | Magpielark
Grallina cyanoleuca

The Magpielark, also colloquially known as 'peewee,' 'Murray magpie' or 'mudlark,' is a conspicuous black-and-white bird which is often seen in cities and towns. Formerly placed in the endemic Australian mud-nest builders, family Grallinidae, together with the White-winged Chough and Apostlebird, recent DNA research has shown that the Magpielark has a closer affinity with the family Monarchidae, the monarch flycatchers. The sexes show very distinct differences in their facial plumage patterns. The male has a white eyebrow and the female a white frontal bib. Pairs mate for life and use the same nest for many years. They are also highly territorial throughout the year and pairs defend their territory. They are generally sedentary but during the winter non-breeding birds form large nomadic flocks.

Feeds mainly on invertebrates, including insects such as grasshoppers, earthworms, freshwater snails, arthropods and spiders. Diet also includes seeds. They are particularly partial to the fresh-water snail *Lymnea tomentosa*, which is the intermediate host for liver fluke, a serious pest of cattle and sheep.

RANGE AND HABITAT: Commonly occurs throughout Australia in open woodland, usually near farm dams, rivers, creeks or billabongs. Also found on surrounding islands and Tasmania. Forages on the ground in the shallow muddy margins of the water, in short grassy areas, parks and gardens.

BREEDING: Breeding occurs between August and February. Males become highly aggressive during that time and may vigorously attack any intruder. Builds a bowl-shaped nest made of mud lined with hair, grass and tree-fibres. Both sexes share in nest-building, incubation and feeding of nestlings.

TRACK NO. 69: Birds duet or perform what is called antiphonal song where males and females coordinate their songs so precisely that it can sound like a solo performance. Distinctive *pee-wee* or *pee-o-wit* or harsher calls *knee-deep-knee-deep-knee-deep* repeated several times.

70 | Silvereye
Zosterops lateralis

The Silvereye, also called the 'white-eye' because of the obvious ring of white feathers around the eye, is the most common and widespread species in Australia. During the breeding season it occurs in pairs, but otherwise it is found in small to large flocks, foraging for insects and fruit. Birds in south-eastern Australia are partial migrants during the winter months when there is a tendency for these populations to migrate to the northern parts of Australia. Birds with much richer tawny-buff flanks are often found among these migratory flocks. These are birds of the Tasmanian race, which have bred in Tasmania and move to more northern districts for winter.

The Silvereye's diet is varied, taking insects, fruit, and berries as well as pollen and nectar. Its fondness for fruit can lead to the birds being both a pest, damaging fruit orchards, and a pest-controller, feeding on insects such as aphids. They are also responsible for spreading weeds such as Bitou Bush, *Lantana* and Small-leaf Privet.

RANGE AND HABITAT: Ranges from the Pascoe River in Queensland down to as far as Eyre Peninsula in South Australia and Tasmania. Also on the south-west coast of Western Australia and on offshore islands. Preferred habitat is open forests, shrubland, gardens and orchards. Familiar visitor to suburban gardens over much of the east, south and south-west.

BREEDING: Breeds from August to January and builds a flimsy little cup-shaped nests from grass, hair and cobwebs. Both birds assist in its construction.

TRACK NO. 70: A musical and warbling song is uttered, often mimicry is included. The male sings loudly from a prominent post in his territory. Their contact calls are a reedy *tsee-tsee* as they flit from bush to bush.

71 | Welcome Swallow
Hirundo neoxena

The Welcome Swallow is an Australasian endemic which is nearly identical to the Barn Swallow of the Northern Hemisphere. It is mostly bluish-black above and pale below with a reddish coloured forehead, throat and breast, but it lacks the Barn Swallow's dark breast-band. It has long pointed wings and a deeply forked tail and its streamlined body is perfectly adapted for the capture of flying insects. It is an insectivorous species that specialises on flying arthropods caught on the wing. They have a rapid and erratic darting and gliding flight when in pursuit of flying insects or when snatching them from the surface of water or on the ground.

After the breeding season and during migration they are often seen in large groups on fence wires or powerlines, communicating with each other with twittering calls. Some populations are sedentary, others migratory, and during the winter birds from Tasmania, South Australia and Victoria migrate northwards, while those in Western Australia and in the northern parts of New South Wales seem to be resident.

RANGE AND HABITAT: Occurs throughout most of Australia, Tasmania and New Zealand. Inhabits open areas, cities, open pasture, grassland, farmland and open woodland, but rarely seen in the inland arid zone and deserts.

BREEDING: Breeds from August to December and builds a distinctive cup-shaped mud nest under a bridge, in a cave or hollow tree, or under the eaves of buildings. The nest is a cup of mud pellets strengthened with pieces of grass and straw and lined with fur, feathers, hair or grass. Studies have shown that they often return to the same nest each year often with the same partner.

TRACK NO. 71: Delicate warbling and twittering song, chatter and whistles usually sung from a perch, but also given in flight.

72 | Fairy Martin
Petrochelidon ariel

Like its close relative the Tree Martin, the Fairy Martin, also called the 'bottle swallow,' has blackish upperparts, whitish underparts and a white rump which is very noticeable in flight. The Fairy Martin, however, has a diagnostic chestnut-brown crown which extends from the forehead to the nape. In the north of Queensland also beware of confusion with the pale-rumped Australian Swiftlet. All of these species are insectivorous and feed on small insects while on the wing.

RANGE AND HABITAT: Occurs in a variety of habitats, including in towns and cities, over most of Australia. Absent only from dry desert regions and Tasmania.

BREEDING: A colonial breeder which nests from August to January. Builds a characteristic domed nest of mud with a spout-like entrance that looks like a bottle. The nest can be situated under bridges or culverts, or on overhanging trees and rock faces above water. The population of this species is considered to be increasing, with the widespread provision of artificial nest-sites possibly a contributing factor.

TRACK NO. 72: Fairy Martin calls are distinctive churring *drr-drr*.

73 | Tree Martin
Petrochelidon nigricans

The Tree Martin is predominantly dark blackish-blue above and pale whitish below, but it lacks the deep rufous throat and long tail-streamers of the Welcome Swallow. Both Tree and Fairy Martins show a white rump which is particularly noticeable in flight, but Tree Martin has a mostly bluish crown, with just a small pale buff patch on the forehead, which is in sharp contrast to the extensive orange-brown crown of the Fairy Martin. Tree Martins are insectivorous and feed on small insects while on the wing. A sociable species which usually occurs in flocks and sometimes associates with Tree Martins and Welcome Swallows.

RANGE AND HABITAT: Breeds across most of Australia except in the dry desert and the far north. Common winter visitor to the far north of Australia, and a widespread breeding visitor to Tasmania, where the Fairy Martin is generally absent.

BREEDING: Colonial breeder nesting from August to January. Usually builds bottle-shaped nest in a hollow limb of a tree.

TRACK NO. 73: A high-pitched trill and a harsh *chuk* call.

74 | Mistletoebird
Dicaeum hirundinaceum

Male dark blue above with red breast and undertail-coverts and white belly. Female and juvenile olive-brown above and whitish below, with a whitish supercilium and orange-buff undertail-coverts.

Forages around mistletoe clumps for insects, nectar, pollen and berries. A highly specialised mutual dependency has developed between the bird and the mistletoe, with the plants relying on the birds to disperse their seeds and the birds relying on the berries for food. The birds are largely responsible for the spread of the 60 or so varieties of mistletoe in Australia.

RANGE AND HABITAT: Found throughout Australia and common in most places where their staple diet of mistletoe berries is to be found.

BREEDING: Breeds between October and March, according to the fruiting of mistletoe. Nest a delicate pear-shaped structure with a side entrance suspended from a thin branch. The female alone builds the nest and incubates the eggs, but both sexes participate in feeding the young.

TRACK NO. 74: A sharp *pretty sweet* and other notes are given and often a soft warbling or mimicry in subsong. Also an accomplished mimic and ventriloquist.

ACKNOWLEDGEMENT

The author would like to thank Roma Kane for her support and comments on an earlier draft of the manuscript.

IMAGE CREDITS

(l=left, r=right, a=above, b=below)

agami.nl: 12r; 23r; 32l; 32r; 33r; 36r; 38l; 44r; 50l

dreamstime.com (individual photographer names in brackets): front cover, 31l, 31r (BG Miner); disk cover (Andrew Downey); back cover top (Peter Sewell); back cover centre, 29l (Grant Phillips); back cover bottom, 18r (Fouroaks); back cover flap (Tracie Louise); 2–3, 57r (John Carnemolla); 6, 43r (Clearviewstock); 8l (Scooperdigital); 8r (Petr Masek); 9l (David Steele); 9r, 11, 17r, 19 (Zambezishark); 10l (Sirichai Dreamstime); 10r, 25l (Thomas Samantzis); 12l (Aussiesnakes); 13l, 54r (Zcello); 13r (Lisa Strachan); 14 (Ecophoto); 15l, 35 (Kristoff Bakkes); 15r (Greenyowie); 16l (Justinrasta); 16r (Zenotri); 17l (Oberstark); 18l (Kazzadev); 20 (Tinamou); 21l (Rubyvale); 21r (Kajornyot); 22l, 22r (Greta van der Rol); 23l (Janecat11); 25r (Marcel Rene Grossman); 26 (JS Mcqueen); 27l (Dean Bertoncelj); 27r, 28r, 33l, 46r, 57l (Feathercollector); 28l, 44l (Ozflash); 29r (Ben Twist); 30 (Nickolay Stanev); 34 (Rossco); 36l (Kathie Thomas); 37l (Steve Broadley); 37r (Mjankor); 38r (Ina van Hateren); 39, 52, 53l (Sarah-Jane Allen); 40 (Robyn Butler); 41r (jtw262); 42l (Rhys Pope); 42r, 45l, 54l, 56 (Houani); 43l (Awcnz62); 46l (Tanya Puntti); 47r (Claret10); 48 (Lucidwaters); 49 (Kevin de Lacy); 50r (Tonympix); 51 (Melva); 53r (Paek0022); 55a (Ksenia Tauroa); 55b (Vickie Priestley)

Simon Papps: 24

Ken Stepnell: 33r, 45r, 58l

Fred van Gessel: front cover flap, 47l

TRACK LISTING

01. **Black Swan** calls, 29/1/1985, Newcastle, NSW.
    Black Swan group calling, 17/10/1999, Dangar Lagoon, Uralla, NSW.
    Black Swan calls, 1/1/1989, Triabanna, Tasmania.
    Black Swan male, female and cygnets, 8/10/2007, Armidale, NSW.

02. **Australian Wood Duck** various calls male and female, 16/7/1988, Woy Woy, NSW.
    Australian Wood Duck in flight, 11/2/2005, Edgar Dam, Tasmania.

03. **Pacific Black Duck** contact calls and Australian Reed-Warbler, 23/9/2009, Mullorina Stn, SA.
    Pacific Black Duck contact calls, 7/3/2009, Smiths Lake, NSW.
    Pacific Black Duck calls and Wandering Whistling-Ducks, 6/10/1984, Palmerston, NT.

04. **Spotted Dove** calling, 8/12/2009, Woy Woy, NSW.
    Spotted Dove call variation, 9/12/2009, Woy Woy, NSW.
    Spotted Dove male song 05122010 Woy Woy, NSW.
    Spotted Dove various courtship calls, 25/8/2012, Woy Woy, NSW.

05. **Crested Pigeon** male display calls, 25/9/1988, Wanaaring, NSW.
    Crested Pigeon courting, 17/11/2007, Leeton, NSW.
    Crested Pigeon in flight, 25/8/2002, Alice Springs, NT.

06. **Tawny Frogmouth** territorial calls, 21/8/2006, Mt Kaputar, NSW.
    Tawny Frogmouth, two birds calling, 7/10/1987, Blackdown Tabletop Mtn, Qld.
    Tawny Frogmouth juv begging, 16/1/2001, Smiths Lake, NSW.

07. **White-faced Heron** calls, 14/8/2001, Mitchell Weir, Qld.
    White-faced Heron calls in flight, Kooragang Island, Newcastle, NSW.

08. **Collared Sparrowhawk** male calling to female, 10/1997, Grampians, Vic.
    Collared Sparrowhawk 11/1982, Barrington NP, NSW.
    Collared Sparrowhawk Immature, 17/2/2005, Blackwater Creek, Tasmania.

09. **Nankeen Kestrel** calls, 12/9/2001, Glen Riddle Dam, NSW.
    Nankeen Kestrel, 3/10/1993, Wugin, WA.
    Nankeen Kestrel, 10/11/2003, Cook, SA.

10. **Peregrine Falcon** adult calling, 19/9/1988, Mootwingee NP, NSW.
    Peregrine Falcon alarm calls, 20/4/2006, Gloucester Tops NP, NSW.
    Peregrine Falcon, two juvs begging, 24/12/2004, Woy Woy, NSW.

11. **Masked Lapwing** male and female contact calls, 6/3/2011, Smiths Lake, NSW.
    Masked Lapwing calls near young, 1/3/2004, Smiths Lake, NSW.
    Masked Lapwing alarm aerial predator, 28/4/2004, Woy Woy, NSW.

12. **Silver Gull** group calls, 19/9/2012, Broughton Island, NSW.

13. **Yellow-tailed Black-cockatoo** call in flight, 1/1997, Talbingo, NSW.
    Yellow-tailed Black-cockatoo calls in flight, 15/2/2005, Strahan, Tasmania.
    Yellow-tailed Black-cockatoo feeding calls, 1/10/1995, Armidale, NSW.
    Yellow-tailed Black-cockatoo single and group calls, 2/4/2009, Penrose, NSW.

14. **Galah** calls, 6/8/2002, Buckinbah Weir, Qld.
    Galah calls 3/6/2007, Frome Waterhole, SA.
    Galah calls in flight, 4/10/1986, Widden Valley, NSW.
    Galah male and female calls, 6/6/2005, Mt Walsh NP, Qld.
    Galah large flock, 28/5/2010, Dig Tree, NSW.
    Galah screeching, 3/10/2014, Woy Woy, NSW.

15. **Little Corella** calls, 18/9/1988, Mootwingee NP, NSW.
    Little Corella contact calls, 15/9/2009, Coongie Lakes, SA.
    Little Corella calls in flight, 17/9/2009, Coongie Lakes, SA.
    Little Corella flock, 10/8/2002, Arthur River, NT.

16. **Sulphur-crested Cockatoo** single calls, 3/10/2007, Utopia, Qld.
    Sulphur-crested Cockatoo alarm calls, 4/1997, Widden Valley, NSW.
    Sulphur-crested Cockatoo group flight, 1/12/2008, Misty Mountains, Qld.
    Sulphur-crested Cockatoo contact calls, 10/10/2014, Woy Woy, NSW.

17. **Rainbow Lorikeet** single bird call, 9/12/2009, Woy Woy, NSW.
    Rainbow Lorikeet calls, 8/2/2011, Woy Woy, NSW.
    Rainbow Lorikeet feeding calls, 10/12/2004, Woy Woy, NSW.
    Rainbow Lorikeet flock, 26/11/2005, Iron Range NP, Qld.

18. **Crimson Rosella** calls, 2/10/1989, Gloucester Tops NP, NSW.
    Crimson Rosella calls in flight, 1/2/2004, Basket Swamp, Tenterfield, NSW.
    Crimson Rosella song, 4/10/1987, Boonoo Boonoo, NSW.
    Crimson Rosella calls, 28/10/1993, Apsley Gorge, NSW.
    Crimson Rosella calls 4/11/2003, Otway NP, Vic.
    Crimson Rosella group calls, 3/10/2014, Gloucester Tops NP, NSW.

19. **Pheasant Coucal** call, 27/12/1993, Mount Lewis, Qld.
    Pheasant Coucal alarm, 19/2/2001, Lizard Island, Qld.
    Pheasant Coucal, 10/1/1993, Smiths Lake, NSW.
    Pheasant Coucal, 19/1/1995, Cameron Beach, NT.
    Pheasant Coucal, 27/12/1993, Kingfisher Park, Qld.
    Pheasant Coucal, 4/12/2008, Mackay, Qld.

20. **Eastern Koel** male calling, 14/10/2002, Smiths Lake, NSW.
    Eastern Koel female calling, 4/1/2008, Woy Woy, NSW.
    Eastern Koel male and female, 3/1/2008, Woy Woy, NSW.
    Eastern Koel male alarm, 24/12/2006, Newcastle, NSW.
    Eastern Koel male and female, 3/2/2008, Woy Woy, NSW.
    Eastern Koel juv begging and Red Wattlebird, 21/1/2008, Woy Woy, NSW.

21. **Channel-billed Cuckoo** three birds calling, 7/11/2000, Smiths Lake, NSW.
    Channel-billed Cuckoo, 5/12/2008, Utopia, Qld.

22. **Shining Bronze-cuckoo** calls, 4/9/1988, Brisbane Waters NP, NSW.
    Shining Bronze-cuckoo calls, 30/7/1988, Wingham, NSW.
    Shining Bronze-cuckoo two males and one female display, 5/10/2008, Clarkesdale NR, Vic.

23. **Fan-tailed Cuckoo** two birds calling, 9/8/1987, Wollombi, NSW.
    Fan-tailed Cuckoo three birds calling, 13/4/2011, Utopia, Qld.
    Fan-tailed Cuckoo single bird calls, 15/8/2006, Flinders Range, SA.

24. **Powerful Owl** male calling, 28/5/1989, Gloucester Tops NP, NSW.
    Powerful Owl female growling, 28/6/1989, Gloucester Tops NP, NSW.
    Powerful Owl juv calling, 28/6/1989, Gloucester Tops NP, NSW.

25. **Southern Boobook** two different calls, 27/1/1996, Gloucester Tops NP, NSW.
    Southern Boobook (Tas subspecies) fast high-pitched calls, 27/2/2005, Paloona, Tas.
    Southern Boobook juv whining call, 14/11/2007, Conimbla NP, NSW.

26. **Eastern Barn Owl** in flight, 2/6/2010, Coopers Ck, Qld.
    Eastern Barn Owl in flight, 20/8/1992, Kakadu NP, NT.
    Eastern Barn Owl juv calls, 20/8/1992, Kakadu NP, NT.

27. **Laughing Kookaburra** greeting calls, 2/8/2004, Dunns Swamp, NSW.
    Laughing Kookaburra calls near nest, 24/12/2005, Julatten, Qld.
    Laughing Kookaburra young in nest, 24/12/2005, Julatten, Qld.
    Laughing Kookaburra attacking Goanna, 19/11/2004, Smiths Lake, NSW.

28. **Blue-winged Kookaburra**

two birds greeting, 10/9/1992, Edith Falls, NT.
Blue-winged Kookaburra morning calls, 4/9/2003, Karijini NP, WA.

29. **Sacred Kingfisher** male territorial calls, 31/10/2006, Deepwater, NSW.
Sacred Kingfisher two adults calling, 14/10/2002, Smiths Lake, NSW.
Sacred Kingfisher calls, 10/1997, Calperum Stn., SA.
Sacred Kingfisher calls, 11/1985, Kapelga, NT.
Sacred Kingfisher greeting calls male and female, 11/1985, Kapelga, NT.
Sacred Kingfisher male and female calling, 11/1985, Kapelga, NT.

30. **Dollarbird** calls, 31/10/2006, Deepwater, NSW.
Dollarbird calls, 5/12/2008, Utopia, Qld.
Dollarbird pair copulating, 24/10/2007, Old Bar, NSW.

31. **Satin Bowerbird** display near bower, 11/11/1996, Eagle Reach, Maitland, NSW.
Satin Bowerbird male scream, 2/11/2007, Woy Woy, NSW.
Satin Bowerbird display, 3/12/1995, Brisbane Waters NP, NSW.
Satin Bowerbird male scream, 27/10/2008, Basket Swamp, Tenterfield, NSW.
Satin Bowerbird display, 11/10/1999, O'Reilly's, Lamington NP, Qld.

32. **Great Bowerbird** calls, 6/12/2005, Wennlock River, Qld.
Great Bowerbird display calls near bower, 6/12/2005, Wennlock River, Qld.
Great Bowerbird calls, 1/11/2002, Lawn Hill NP, Qld.

33. **Superb Fairy-wren** male calling, 15/9/1979, Warwick, Qld.
Superb Fairy-wren calls, 3/10/2000, Bathurst, NSW.
Superb Fairy-wren alarm calls, 18/9/2003, Warrumbungles NP, NSW.
Superb Fairy-wren calls, 5/6/1988, Wollombi, NSW.

34. **Variegated Fairy-wren** song and alarm, 22/9/1982, Mootwingee NP, NSW.
Variegated Fairy-wren warning calls, 3/3/2006, Smiths Lake, NSW.
Variegated Fairy-wren alarm, 4/6/1988, Wollombi, NSW.
Variegated Fairy-wren male song, 8/1982, Dudley, Newcastle, NSW.

35. **White-browed Scrubwren** male song, 4/6/1988, Wollombi, NSW.
White-browed Scrubwren male display song, 2/10/2007, Utopia, Qld.
White-browed Scrubwren male and female song, 5/8/2009, Utopia, Qld.
White-browed Scrubwren warning calls, 23/8/2015, Warrumbungles NP, NSW.

36. **Yellow-rumped Thornbill** song phrases, 4/1979, Maitland, NSW.
Yellow-rumped Thornbill song, 7/1998, Simpson Gap NR, NT.
Yellow-rumped Thornbill song, 9/1982, Mootwingee NP, NSW.
Yellow-rumped Thornbill song, 8/12/2006, Millicent, SA.
Yellow-rumped Thornbill song near nest, 9/11/2003, Walgunya Cons Pk, SA.
Yellow-rumped Thornbill calls, 15/8/2006, Flinders Range, SA.

37. **Brown Thornbill** territorial display call, 9/8/1987, Wollombi, NSW.
Brown Thornbill song, 17/3/2009, Langothlan Lagoon, NSW.
Brown Thornbill song, 7/6/2010, Southwood NP, Qld.
Brown Thornbill contact calls, 5/11/2003, Glenelg NP, Vic.
Brown Thornbill contact calls, 4/11/2003, Otway NP, Vic.
Brown Thornbill hawk alarm, 4/9/1988, Woy Woy, NSW.

38. **Spotted Pardalote** male display song, 11/1978, Wollombi, NSW.
Spotted Pardalote male display song, 4/10/2008, Clarkesdale NR, Vic.
Spotted Pardalote male calls, 26/3/2008, Brisbane Waters NP, NSW.
Spotted Pardalote contact calls, 26/3/2002, Kanungra Walls, NSW.
Spotted Pardalote contact calls, 4/5/2003, Gluepot Res, SA.

39. **Striated Pardalote** male display, 5/10/2012, Langothlan Lagoon, NSW.
Striated Pardalote territorial calls, 5/8/2002, Boggabri, NSW.
Striated Pardalote contact calls, 1/10/1994, Round Hill NR, NSW.
Striated Pardalote contact calls, 30/9/2007, Utopia, Qld.
Striated Pardalote contact calls, 9/10/1987, Eungella, Qld.
Striated Pardalote contact calls, 2/5/2003, Gluepot Res, SA.
Striated Pardalote contact calls, 15/8/2006, Flinders Range, SA.
Striated Pardalote contact calls, 24/7/2004, White Wells Stn, WA.

40. **Eastern Spinebill** calls, 3/10/1996, Warrumbungles NP, NSW.
Eastern Spinebill song, 16/7/1988, Patonga, NSW.
Eastern Spinebill song, 22/3/1987, Gloucester Tops NP, NSW.
Eastern Spinebill calls, 23/8/2005, Tenterfield, NSW.
Eastern Spinebill song, 12/1998, Lake Tyre, Vic.
Eastern Spinebill calls, 19/9/2008, Tenterfield, NSW.

41. **Western Spinebill** calls, 29/9/1993, Dryandra NP, WA.
Western Spinebill display flight male and female, 16/11/2003, Fitzgerald NP, WA.
Western Spinebill calls, 24/9/1993, Stirling Range, WA.

42. **Lewin's Honeyeater** different songs, 22/8/2005, Lamington NP, Qld.
Lewin's Honeyeater song, 28/5/2000, Wollombi, NSW.
Lewin's Honeyeater calls, 5/3/2006, Smiths lake, NSW.
Lewin's Honeyeater song, 1/3/2004, Smiths Lake, NSW.
Lewin's Honeyeater alarm and song, 3/3/2012, Smiths Lake, NSW.

43. **Singing Honeyeater** dawn calls, 7/9/2009, Gundabooka NP, Qld.
Singing Honeyeater calls, 3/9/1993, White Springs, NT.
Singing Honeyeater dawn song, 4/9/1998, Broome, WA.
Singing Honeyeater long trill, 3/7/1998, Tanami H'way, NT.

44. **Yellow-faced Honeyeater** dawn calls, 23/12/1989, Moonbi Range, NSW.
Yellow-faced Honeyeater calls and song, 7/8/1994, Wollombi, NSW.
Yellow-faced Honeyeater male song, 3/8/2009, Blackdown Tabletop NP, Qld.
Yellow-faced Honeyeater calls on migration, 25/5/1991, Ourimbah SF, NSW.

45. **White-plumed Honeyeater** chick-o-weet calls, 1/10/1991, Mootwingee NP, NSW.
White-plumed Honeyeater dawn song, 8/9/1982, Coopers Creek, NSW.
White-plumed Honeyeater alarm calls, 6/8/2006, Nappa Marie Stn, Qld.
White-plumed Honeyeater flight song, 27/5/2007, Betoota Cons Pk, Qld.
White-plumed Honeyeater display flight, 5/5/2003, Lake Cullurellaine, Vic.
White-plumed Honeyeater alarm calls, 10/1997, Goulbourne NP, NSW.

46. **Noisy Miner** dawn calls, 1/10/2007, Utopia, Qld.
Noisy Miner contact calls, 4/1997, Widden Valley, NSW.
Noisy Miner contact calls, 4/1997, Widden Valley, NSW.
Noisy Miner scolding calls, 4/1997, Widden Valley, NSW.
Noisy Miner group alarm, 16/10/2014, Woy Woy, NSW.

47. **Little Wattlebird** male display song, 11/8/2011, Patonga, NSW.
Little Wattlebird dawn calls, 3/10/2010, Woy Woy, NSW.
Little Wattlebird male calling, 25/2/2005, St Helens, Tasmania.
Western Wattlebird song, 17/11/2003, Fitzgerald NP, WA.

48. **Red Wattlebird** male predawn song, 9/9/2012, Woy Woy, NSW.
Red Wattlebird female and male calls, 10/6/2004, Woy Woy, NSW.
Red Wattlebird single calls, 22/6/2011, Woy Woy, NSW.
Red Wattlebird male and female dispute, 12/12/2007, Woy Woy, NSW.
Red Wattlebird group contact, feeding and dispute, 6/1999, Katoomba, NSW.

49. **Brown Honeyeater** song, 3/10/1996, Warrumbungles NP, NSW.
Brown Honeyeater calls, 9/7/2004, Rabbit Flat, NT.
Brown Honeyeater territorial song, 10/6/2007, Quilpie, Qld.
Brown Honeyeater territorial song, 18/9/1993, Stirling Range NP, WA.

50. **New Holland Honeyeater** song, 7/1983, Newcastle, NSW.
New Holland Honeyeater contact calls, 2/7/1988, Patonga, NSW.
New Holland Honeyeater song, 22/2/2005, Bruny Island, Tasmania.
New Holland Honeyeater group alarm, 7/10/1997, Little Desert, SA.

51. **Noisy Friarbird** calls, 26/12/2009, Smiths Lake, NSW.
Noisy Friarbird calls, 9/8/1987, Wollombi, NSW.
Noisy Friarbird calls, 18/9/2003, Warrumbungles NP, NSW.
Noisy Friarbird song, 23/8/2006, Warrumbungles NP, NSW.
Noisy Friarbird song, 27/4/1996, Forbes, NSW.

52. **Blue-faced Honeyeater** juv contact calls, 18/8/2001, Quilpie, Qld.
Blue-faced Honeyeater dawn calls, 25/8/1984, Kakadu NP, NT.
Blue-faced Honeyeater contact calls, 12/12/2005, Wennlock River, Qld.
Blue-faced Honeyeater contact calls, 9/8/1987, Wollombi, NSW.

53. **Black-faced Cuckoo-shrike** different calls, 9/9/1999, Woy Woy, NSW.
Black-faced Cuckoo-shrike calls, 19/9/2003, Warrumbungles NP, NSW.
Black-faced Cuckoo-shrike dispute, 20/9/1993, Stirling Range, WA.
Black-faced Cuckoo-shrike song, 6/6/1985, Darwin, NT.
Black-faced Cuckoo-shrike calls, 20/8/2001, Dig Tree, Qld.
Black-faced Cuckoo-shrike contact calls, 30/9/1993, Dryandry NP, WA.

54. **White-bellied Cuckoo-shrike** song, 1/1998, Smiths Lake, NSW.
White-bellied Cuckoo-shrike calls, 10/1980, Warrumbungles NP, NSW.
White-bellied Cuckoo-shrike calls, 12/12/2005, Wenlock River, Qld.
White-bellied Cuckoo-shrike contact calls, 24/12/1995, Townsville, Qld.

55. **Grey Shrike-thrush** song, 10/6/2007, Eromangee, Qld.
Grey Shrike-thrush song, 14/4/2009, Patonga, NSW.
Grey Shrike-thrush song, 10/8/2009, Cathedral Rock, NSW.
Grey Shrike-thrush duet, 12/7/2009, Lake Constance, Qld.
Grey Shrike-thrush courtship, 15/8/2006, Flinders Range, SA.
Grey Shrike-thrush calls, 6/7/2005, Patonga, NSW.
Grey Shrike-thrush winter call, 15/4/1995, Widden Valley, NSW.

56. **Green Figbird** group song at dawn, 7/11/2009, Smiths Lake, NSW.
Green Figbird song, 10/10/2009, Woy Woy, NSW.
Green Figbird calls and song, 11/1998, Smiths Lake, NSW.
Green Figbird *chipp* calls, 1/11/2006, Newcastle, NSW.

57. **Yellow Oriole** male and female song, 27/11/2008, Coen, Qld.
Yellow Oriole male song, 5/4/1985, Fogg Dam, NT.
Yellow Oriole male territorial song, 13/11/2002, Iron Range NP, Qld.
Yellow Oriole song, 8/11/1990, Ingham, Qld.
Yellow Oriole song, 20/10/1987, Daintree, Qld.

58. **Olive-backed Oriole** song, 26/12/2009, Smiths Lake, NSW.
Olive-backed Oriole male calling, 2/11/2003, Mimosa NP, Vic.
Olive-backed Oriole calls, 12/1996, Kosciuszko NP, NSW.
Olive-backed Oriole mimicry, 23/8/2006, Warrumbungles NP, NSW.

59. **Black Butcherbird** song, 20/1/1985, Darwin, NT.
Black Butcherbird two birds calling, 19/1/1985, Cameron Beach, NT.
Black Butcherbird calls, 1/1/1994, Atherton Tablelands, Qld.
Black Butcherbird calls, 9/1979, Mission Beach, Qld.
Black Butcherbird dawn song male and female, 22/11/2002, Iron Range NP, Qld.

60. **Grey Butcherbird** song, 2/1997, Smiths Lake, NSW.
Grey Butcherbird duet, 12/9/1987, Patterson, NSW.
Grey Butcherbird territorial song, 1/10/1994, Round Hill NR, NSW.
Grey Butcherbird warning calls, 5/5/2003, Mildura, Vic.
Grey Butcherbird calls, 9/11/2003, Walgunyah Cons Pk, SA.
Grey Butcherbird song, 14/8/2006, Gammon Range, SA.
Grey Butcherbird song, 27/7/2004, Southern Cross, WA.
Grey Butcherbird dawn calls, 8/7/2004, Mt Wedge, NT.

61. **Pied Butcherbird** duet, 24/6/1984, Daly River, NT.
Pied Butcherbird single calls, 11/1996, Maitland, NSW.
Pied Butcherbird alarm calls, 12/1983, Kakadu NP, NT
Pied Butcherbird calls, 14/8/2006, Gammon Range, SA.

62. **Australian Magpie** song 2am, 9/1982, Mootwingee NP, NSW.
Australian Magpie single calls, 15/8/2006, Flinders Range, SA.
Australian Magpie duet, 27/6/2006, Woy Woy, NSW.
Australian Magpie dawn male and female, 20/7/1988, Wingham, NSW.

63. **Spangled Drongo** song, 2/12/2005, Iron Range NP, Qld.
Spangled Drongo calls, 28/12/1993, Julatten, Qld.
Spangled Drongo mimicry, 8/8/1992, Fogg Dam, NT.
Spangled Drongo duet, 8/12/2005, Punsand Bay, Qld.
Spangled Drongo mimicry, 3/1/2006, Mt Carbine, Qld.

64. **Pied Currawong** song, 18/10/2003, Barren Grounds NR, NSW.
Pied Currawong calls, 11/1982, Barrington Tops NP, NSW.
Pied Currawong attack calls, 7/11/2005, Tenterfield, NSW.
Pied Currawong calls, 26/11/2008, Coen, Qld.
Pied Currawong group song, 22/4/2007, Woy Woy, NSW.

65. **Grey Fantail** song, 17/11/2003, Fitzgerald NP, WA.
Grey Fantail song, 27/11/2000, Smiths Lake, NSW.
Grey Fantail song, 19/9/1993, Stirling Range NP, WA.
Grey Fantail song and calls, 24/7/2004 White Wells Stn, WA.
Grey Fantail song, 25/10/2006, Tenterfield, NSW.

66. **Willie Wagtail** dawn song, 6/8/2006, Coopers Creek, Qld.
Willie Wagtail territorial song, 30/7/1998, Meteorite Crater, NT.
Willie Wagtail warning calls, 13/1/2001, Smiths Lake, NSW.
Willie Wagtail alarm calls, 31/5/2002, Woy Woy, NSW.
Willie Wagtail alarm calls, 2/6/2007, Frome Waterhole, SA.

67. **Australian Raven** calls, 7/4/1995, Patonga, NSW.
Australian Raven calls, 15/8/2006, Flinders Range, SA.
Australian Raven calls, 3/6/2007, Frome Waterhole, SA.
Australian Raven calls, 10/6/2007, Eromangee, Qld.
Australian Raven calls, 18/5/2005, Tenterfield, NSW.

68. **Torresian Crow** calls, 9/1979, Brisbane, Qld.
Torresian Crow alarm, 7/2/2004, Brisbane, Qld.
Torresian Crow calls, 28/7/1984, Reynolds River, NT.
Torresian Crow calls, 5/6/2005, Blackdown Tabletop Mtn, Qld.
Torresian Crow calls, 22/11/2008, Wennlock River, Qld.

69. **Magpielark** contact call, 16/1/2007, Newcastle, NSW.
Magpielark contact call, 19/2/2007, Newcastle, NSW.
Magpielark calls, 1/1/1984, Victoria River Crossing, NT.
Magpielark song, 17/3/2009, Langothlin NR, NSW.
Magpielark male and female song, 13/10/2003, Narooma, Vic.
Magpielark male display call, 11/9/2001, Glen Riddle Dam, NSW.

70. **Silvereye** song, 3/11/1991, Newcastle, NSW.
Silvereye contact calls, 13/4/2011, Utopia, Qld.
Silvereye contact calls, 4/3/2011, Smiths Lake, NSW.
Silvereye alarm near nest, 2/7/1988, Patonga, NSW.
Silvereye contact call on migration, 18/5/2003, Woy Woy, NSW.

71. **Welcome Swallow** song, 6/8/2002, Buckinbah Weir, Qld.
Welcome Swallow courtship song, 10/11/2003, Cook, SA.
Welcome Swallow alarm calls, 22/5/2001, Muswellbrook, NSW.

72. **Fairy Martin** calls near nests, 7/10/1995, Capertee Valley, NSW.

73. **Tree Martin** song, 27/8/2002, Menindee, Qld.
Tree Martin calls, 14/9/2001, Borah Res, WA.
Tree Martin calls, 16/8/2001, Ward River, Qld.

74. **Mistletoebird** male song, mimicry and calls, 29/3/2007, Patonga, NSW.
Mistletoebird male song, 9/1982, Mootwingee NP, NSW.
Mistletoebird male song, 13/10/1997, Pooncarie, NSW.
Mistletoebird calls, 7/8/2002, Barcaldine, Qld.
Mistletoebird calls, 10/6/2007, Eromangee, Qld.

BIBLIOGRAPHY

BOOKS

Angel, T. 1986. *Ravens, Crows, Magpies and Jays*. University of Washington Press.

Barrett,G.,Silcocks, A., Barry,S., Cunningham,R. and Poulter,R. 2003. *The New Atlas of Australian Birds*. Birds Australia (Royal Australasian Ornithologists Union).

Beruldsen, G. 1980. *A Field Guide to Nest and Eggs of Australian Birds*. Rigby Publishers Limited, Adelaide.

Blakers, M., Davies, S.J.J.F. and Reilly, P.N. 1984. *The Atlas of Australian Birds*. Royal Australian Ornithologists Union. Melbourne University Press.

Burton, J. and Taylor, K. 1983. *Nightwatch, The Natural World from Dusk to Dawn*. Roxby Nightwatch Limited.

Burton, J. A. 1985. *Owls of the World, Their Evolution, Structure and Ecology*. Hodder and Stoughton, Sydney.

Cameron, A. 2007. *Cockatoos*. CSIRO Publishing, Collingwood.

Catterall, C.P., Driscoll,P.V., Hulsman, K., Muir, D. and Taplin, A. 1993. *Birds in their Habitats: Status and Conservation in Queensland*. Queensland Ornithological Society Inc.

Christides, L. and Boles, W.E. 2008. *Systematics and Taxonomy of Australian Birds*. CSIRO Publishing, Collingwood.

Cooper, W.T. and Hindwood, K. 1961. *A Portfolio of Australian Birds*. A.H. & A.W. Reed, Sydney.

Cooper, W.T. and Forshaw, J.M. 1977. *The Birds of Paradise and Bower Birds*. Collins, Sydney.

Erritzoe, J., Mann, C.F., Brammer, F.P. and Fuller, R.A. 2012. *Cuckoos of the World*. Christopher Helm, London.

Feare, C. and Craig, A. 1998. *Starlings and Mynas*. Christopher Helm, London.

Fleay, D. 1968. *Nightwatchman of Bush and Plains*. The Jacaranda Press.

Forshaw, J.M. and Cooper, W.T. 1985. *Australian Parrots* (2nd Ed.). Landsdowne Press, Melbourne.

Frazer, I. and Gray, J. 2013. *Australian Bird Names: A complete Guide*. CSIRO Publishing, Collingwood.

Frith, H.J. 1968. *Waterfowl in Australia* (reprint). Angus and Robertson Ltd, Sydney.

Frith, H.J. 1976. *Birds in the Australian High Country*. A.H. & A.W. Reed, Sydney.

Frith, H.J. 1982. *Pigeons and Doves of Australia*. Rigby Publishers, Adelaide.

Goodwin, D. 1970. *Pigeons and Doves of the World* (2nd Ed.). Trustees of the British Museum (Natural History), London.

Gotch, A.F. 1981. *Birds: Their Latin Names Explained*. Blandford Press.

Hancock, J. and Kushlan, J. 1984. *The Herons Handbook*. Croom Helm, London and Sydney.

Higgins, P.J. and Davies, P. 1996. *Handbook of Australian, New Zealand and Antarctic Birds. Vol.3: Snipe to Pigeons*. Oxford University Press, Melbourne.

Higgins, P.J. 1999. *Handbook of Australian, New Zealand and Antarctic Birds. Vol.4: Parrots to Dollarbird*. Oxford University Press, Melbourne.

Higgins, P.J., Peter, J.M. and Steele, W.K. 2001. *Handbook of Australian, New Zealand and Antarctic Birds. Vol.5: Tyrant Flycatchers to Chats*. Oxford University Press, Melbourne.

Higgins, P.J. and Peter, J.M. 2002. *Handbook of Australian, New Zealand and Antarctic Birds. Vol.6: Pardalotes to Shrike-thrushes*. Oxford University Press, Melbourne.

Higgins, P.J., Peter, J.M. and Cowling, S.J. 2006. *Handbook of Australian, New Zealand and Antarctic Birds. Vol.7, Part A: Boatbill to Larks*. Oxford University Press, Melbourne.

Higgins, P.J., Peter, J.M. and Cowling, S.J. 2006. *Handbook of Australian, New Zealand and Antarctic Birds. Vol.7, Part B: Dunnock to Starlings*. Oxford University Press, Melbourne.

Hindwood, K.A. and McGill. A.R. 1958. *The Birds of Sydney*. The Royal Zoological Society of NSW.

Hollands, D. 1991. *Birds of the Night: Owls, Frogmouths and Nightjars of Australia*. Reed Books Pty. Ltd.

Hollands, D. 2008. *Owls, Frogmouths and Nightjars of Australia*. Bloomings Books.

Kloot, T., McCulloch, E.M. and Trusler, P. 1980. *Birds of Australian Gardens*. Rigby Publishers Pty, Adelaide.

Lendon, A.H. 1979. *Australian Parrots in Field and Aviary*. (Revised Ed.). Angus and Robertson Publishers, Australia.

MacDonald, J.D. 1973. *Birds of Australia. A summary of Information*. A.H. & A.W. Reed, Sydney.

MacDonald, J.D. 1980. *Birds for Beginners. How Birds Live and Behave*. Reed Books.

Marchant, S. and Higgins, P.J. 1993. *Handbook of Australian, New Zealand and Antarctic Birds. Vol.2: Raptors to Lapwings*. Oxford University Press, Melbourne.

Mikkola, H. 2012. *Owls of the World, A Photographic Guide*. Firefly Books, Inc.

Officer, H.R. 1964. *Australian Honeyeaters*. The Bird Observers Club, Melbourne.

Pizzey, G. and Doyle, R. 1980. *Field Guide to the Birds of Australia*. Collins.

Pizzey, G. and Knight, F. 2002. *The Field Guide to the Birds of Australia*. Angus and Robertson.

Reader's Digest. 1976. *Complete Book of Australian Birds* (1st Ed.) Reader's Digest Services Pty Ltd, NSW.

Reader's Digest. 1997. *Encyclopedia of Australian Wildlife*. Reader's Digest, Sydney

Rowland, P. 2008. *Bowerbirds*. CSIRO Publishing, Collingwood.

Rowley, I. 1975. *Bird Life (The Australian Natural Library)*. Taplinger Publishing Co. Inc., New York.

Rowley, I. and Russell, E. 1997. *Fairy-wrens and Grasswrens*. Oxford University Press, New York.

Schoode, R. 1982. *The Fairy Wrens, A Monograph of the* Maluridae. Landsdowne Editions (A Division of R.P.L.A.), Melbourne.

Serventy, D.L. and Whittell, H.M. 1967. *Birds of Western Australia*. Lamb Publications Pty Ltd, Perth.

Serventy, V.N. and McGill, A.R. 1982. *The Wrens and Warblers of Australia*. The National Photographic Index of Australian Wildlife. Angus and Robertson Publications.

Simpson, K. and Day, N. 1999. *Field Guide to the Birds of Australia*. (6th Ed.). Penguin Books Australia Ltd.

Simpson, K. and Wilson, Z. 1998. *Birdwatching in Australia and New Zealand*. Reed New Holland.

Slater, P., Slater, P. and Slater, R. 2003. *The Slater Field Guide to Australian Birds*. New Holland Publishers (Australia) Ltd., Sydney.

Storr, G.M. and Johnstone, R.E. 1979. *Field Guide to the Birds of West Australia*. Western Australian Museum, Perth.

Strahan, R. and Boles, W. 1988. *The Robins and Flycatchers of Australia*. The National Photographic Index of Australian Wildlife. Angus and Robertson Publishers.

Watts. D. 2002. *Field Guide to Tasmanian Birds*. Reed New Holland.

Weaver, P. 1981. *The Bird Watcher's Dictionary*. T & A.D. Poyser.

MAGAZINE/JOURNAL ARTICLES

Boland, C. 2004. Bird Brains. *Nature Australia* 27(11): 46-53.

Christides, L. and Holderness, T. 1998. A Miner Challenge. *Nature Australia* 25(12): 32-39.

Cilento, N. 1997. Dr. Jekyll with the pied hyde. *Nature Australia* 25(10): 32-39.

Dow, D.D. 1977. Indiscriminate interspecific aggression leading to almost sole occupancy of space by a single species of bird. *Emu* 77: 115-121.

Ford, J. 1963. Breeding behaviour in the Yellow-tailed Thornbill in south-western Australia. *Emu* 63: 185-200.

Hall, M. 2003. To kill a Kookaburra. *Nature Australia* 27(7): 52-58.

Kaplan, G. 2003. Magpie mimicry. *Nature Australia* 27(10): 60-67.

Keast, J.A. 1968. Seasonal movements in the Australian honeyeaters (Meliphagidae) and their ecological significance. *Emu* 67: 159-209.

Langmore, N. 2004. Canny cuckoos and wily wrens. *Nature Australia* 28(1): 52-59.

Legge, S. 2002. To kill a Kookaburra. *Nature Australia* 27(5): 27-35.

Magrath, M. 1997. The politics of parenting: an avian perspective. *Nature Australia* 25(9): 58-65.

Major, R. 2003. Urban Currawong. *Nature Australia* 27(9): 53-59.

Mulder, R. and Kraaijeveld, K. 2004. Curley Cues. *Nature Australia* 27(12): 34-43.

Paton, D.C., and H.A. Ford. 1977. Pollination by birds of native plants in South Australia. *Emu* 77: 73-85.

Paton, D.C. 1980. The importance of manna, honeydew and lerp in the diets of honeyeaters. *Emu* 80: 213-226.

Peters, A. 2002. The Burden of beauty. *Nature Australia* 27(6): 30-37.

Robinson, A. 1947. Magpie-Larks, a study in behaviour. *Emu* 46: 265-281 and 382-391.

Rowley, I. 1965. The life history of the Suprb Blue Wren, *Malurus cyaneus*. *Emu* 64: 251-297.

Rowley, I. 1994. 'What a galah'. *Nature Australia* 24(8): 22-29.

Sauders, D.A. 1979. Distribution and taxonomy of the White-tailed and Yellow-tailed Black-Cockatoos *Calyptorhynchus* spp. *Emu* 79: 215-227.

Sinden, K. and Jones, D. 2004. Crows in the City. *Nature Australia* 28(2): 36-43.

Tingay, S. 1974. Antiphonal song of the Magpie Lark. *Emu* 74: 11-17.

Vallenga, R.E. 1970. Behaviour of the male Satin Bowerbird at the bower. *Australian Bird Bander* 8: 3-11.

Van Dyck, S. 1993. Pies from the sky. *Nature Australia* 24(6): 14-15.

Van Dyck, S. 1996. Wrens through theye of a sceptic. *Nature Australia* 25(7): 18-19.

Van Dyck, S. 2002. Fowl Play. *Nature Australia* 27(4): 20-21.

Van Dyck, S. 2003. Kamikazi Cuckoos. *Nature Australia* 27(8): 24-25.

Van Dyck, S. 2005. Miner misdemeanours. *Nature Australia* 28(7): 18-19.

Woinarski, J.C.Z. 1974. A comparison of the ground-nesting of two species of pardalote. *Emu* 74: 219-222.

REFERENCES

Names and the sequence of classification follow those as outlined by Christides and Boles (2008) in the *Systematics and Taxonomy of Australian Birds*.

INDEX

TRACK NUMBER IN BOLD
PAGE NUMBER IN ROMAN

Australian Magpie **62**, 49
Australian Raven **67**, 53
Australian Wood Duck **02**, 9
Black Butcherbird **59**, 47
Black-faced Cuckoo-shrike **53**, 44
Black Swan **01**, 8
Blue-faced Honeyeater **52**, 43
Blue-winged Kookaburra **28**, 27
Brown Honeyeater **49**, 41
Brown Thornbill **37**, 33
Channel-billed Cuckoo **21**, 22
Collared Sparrowhawk **08**, 12
Crested Pigeon **05**, 10
Crimson Rosella **18**, 20
Dollarbird **30**, 28
Eastern Barn Owl **26**, 25
Eastern Koel **20**, 21
Eastern Spinebill **40**, 36
Fairy Martin **72**, 57
Fan-tailed Cuckoo **23**, 23
Galah **14**, 17
Great Bowerbird **32**, 30
Green Figbird **56**, 45
Grey Butcherbird **60**, 47
Grey Fantail **65**, 51

Grey Shrike-thrush **55**, 45
Laughing Kookaburra **27**, 26
Lewin's Honeyeater **42**, 37
Little Corella **15**, 17
Little Wattlebird **47**, 40
Magpielark **69**, 54
Masked Lapwing **11**, 14
Mistletoebird **74**, 58
Nankeen Kestrel **09**, 13
New Holland Honeyeater **50**, 42
Noisy Friarbird **51**, 43
Noisy Miner **46**, 39
Olive-backed Oriole **58**, 46
Pacific Black Duck **03**, 9
Peregrine Falcon **10**, 13
Pheasant Coucal **19**, 21
Pied Butcherbird **61**, 48
Pied Currawong **64**, 50
Powerful Owl **24**, 24
Rainbow Lorikeet **17**, 19
Red Wattlebird **48**, 41
Sacred Kingfisher **29**, 27
Satin Bowerbird **31**, 29
Shining Bronze-cuckoo **22**, 23
Silver Gull **12**, 15
Silvereye **70**, 55
Singing Honeyeater **43**, 37
Southern Boobook **25**, 25

Spangled Drongo **63**, 50
Spotted Dove **04**, 10
Spotted Pardalote **38**, 34
Striated Pardalote **39**, 35
Sulphur-crested Cockatoo **16**, 18
Superb Fairy-wren **33**, 31
Tawny Frogmouth **06**, 11
Torresian Crow **68**, 53
Tree Martin **73**, 57
Variegated Fairy-wren **34**, 32
Welcome Swallow **71**, 56
Western Spinebill **41**, 36
White-bellied Cuckoo-shrike **54**, 44
White-browed Scrubwren **35**, 32
White-faced Heron **07**, 12
White-plumed Honeyeater **45**, 38
Willie Wagtail **66**, 52
Yellow Oriole **57**, 46
Yellow-faced Honeyeater **44**, 38
Yellow-rumped Thornbill **36**, 33
Yellow-tailed Black-cockatoo **13**, 16